LUTHERAN
VOICES

Signs of Belonging
Luther's Marks of the Church and the Christian Life

Mary E. Hinkle

Augsburg Fortress
Minneapolis

SIGNS OF BELONGING:
Luther's Marks of the Church and the Christian Life

Editor: Mark Hinton

Cover design: Koechel Peterson and Associates, Inc., Minneapolis, MN
                www.koechelpeterson.com

Cover photo: Baptismal Font, Prince of Peace Lutheran Church, Burnsville, MN

ISBN 0-8066-4997-6

The paper used in this publication meets the minimum requirements of American National Standard for Information Sciences—Permanence of Paper for Printed Library Materials, ANSI Z329.48-1984.

Manufactured in the U.S.A.

07   06   05   04   03   1   2   3   4   5   6   7   8   9   10

Signs of Belonging
Luther's Marks of the Church and the Christian Life

Contents

Acknowledgments

The idea for this book came from a conversation with *Lutheran Woman Today* editor Nancy Goldberger. Nancy asked me about how Lutherans might talk about measures of success in their Christian faith, and I balked. "Too much of God's work in the world is hidden," I said, "and even though we are part of the new creation, too much of the old sinful self is alive and well for most Lutheran theologians to have any confidence in listing measures of success. We just don't think that way."

Nancy and I talked a while longer, and I remembered a different list, from no less a Lutheran theologian than Martin Luther himself. Luther had listed seven marks of the church, seven public signs of a Christian holy people on earth. They were not measures of success, to be sure, but they were visible and public, and they put the emphasis where Lutherans would want it, on the work of the Holy Spirit to make people holy, rather than on our own effort to achieve holiness. Maybe the marks of the church would offer a way to talk not just about a congregation of Christian holy people, but also about individual Christians and their life of faith. By the end of that phone conversation, I had agreed to write an article on the topic.

The promised article eventually had to be renegotiated because it was growing into this book. I thank Nancy and the rest of the editorial staff at *Lutheran Woman Today* for a question that fueled so much discovery and ongoing conversation. Thanks also to another editor, Scott Tunseth of Augsburg Fortress, for the encouragement to publish the project in Augsburg's *Lutheran Voices* series. The series aims to provide resources for a thoughtful, informed, and inspired Christian faith and I am honored to be part of it.

Finally, I am grateful to the members of my 2002-03 discipleship group at Luther Seminary for conversation on some of the chapters as they were being written and to my teaching assistant, Kyle Fever, for help preparing the manuscript.

1

Where Is the Church? Signs of Belonging

Sometimes when I go to church, I look around at the people gathered, and I want to ask, "Why are you here? Why do you come *here* on Sunday morning instead of sleeping in, or reading the paper, or going for a walk? What are you finding here? How does this place and what happens in it connect to anything else in your life?"

Signs of Belonging explores the connections between the life of a congregation and the daily lives of individual Christians. In spite of the fact that my question, "Why are you here?" usually surfaces at times when church seems crushingly dull or hopelessly silly to me, I know that what happens in congregational life changes the personal, daily lives of those who participate in it. Those who are regularly connected with a community of Christians come to be defined and deepened by a congregation and its common life. This book explores how that happens. What does a flawed fellowship of Christians bring to those who participate in it? How do the practices that are specific to church life—things like sermons, sacraments, and public praying—shape those who participate in them?

Near the end of a long treatise from 1539, Martin Luther numbers what he calls signs or marks of the church. The Apostles' Creed testifies "that a Christian holy people is to be and to remain on earth until the end of the world."[1] Luther asks where to find the "one, holy, catholic and apostolic church" on earth.

Where on earth are such people and how may they be recognized? Are there any clues to the identity of that Christian holy people? "How will or how can a poor confused person tell where such Christian holy people are to be found in this world?"[2]

Perhaps you know the experience of that "poor confused person." Whether one is speaking of life in the 16th century or the 21st, it is not easy to pick Christians out of a crowd. We might wish that Christian behavior demonstrated love for God and neighbor in such an exemplary way that people could say, "Those Christians, how they love one another," or "Look at all the good those people are doing for Christ" (cf. Philemon 1:6). But love and good works are certainly not the sole province of Christians. People of varying faiths or no faith convictions at all are able to show love and do good work. What is more, Christians are as liable to fail in these things as anyone else. Luther does not offer a catalog of virtues as a way to identify a Christian holy people.

Nor does he offer a list of doctrinal or confessional statements as the identifying marks of the church. We have here no list of "spiritual laws" to which Christians must give assent, or statements of faith by which we differentiate God's Christian holy people from everyone else. Even the creeds of the church, as important as they were to the reformers, are not in Luther's list of distinguishing marks of the church. This list of signs pointing to the presence of the church in the world contains no checklist for doctrinal purity.

So if we do not look to ethical behavior or doctrinal purity to differentiate the church from its surroundings, how may a poor confused person recognize a Christian holy people in the world? Martin Luther offers seven pieces of external evidence for locating the church on earth. Where these signs are, there is the church; there are holy people of God.

The list includes seven congregational practices or activities. He uses a play on words, calling these signs "holy possessions," a word also used for relics of the saints in the Catholic church. Medieval churches often placed great value on physical evidence of saints such as bone chips, teeth, or hair, regarding these materials as having wonder-working properties. Luther uses words that describe this physical evidence, but he presses the terms into service to describe the public practices of the gathered people of God rather than the contents of church reliquaries.

Each practice—each sign—is both public and visible. By public, I mean that each sign is accessible to believers and nonbelievers alike. The church is not a secret society. Nor is it solely a mystical reality, invisible on earth except to "the eyes of faith." No. The Holy Spirit makes each sign possible, yet none of them is so mystical as to be hidden from the human eye. The signs are public pointers to the work God does on earth to gather God's people together and make them holy.

Each of the signs has its roots in Scripture. Here is a list of the signs followed by a short description of how each is connected to the Bible and the earliest history of the church.

1. The Word
2. Holy Baptism
3. Holy Communion
4. The Forgiveness and Reproof of Sin
5. The Office of the Ministry
6. Worship, or Public Prayer
7. The Holy Cross (that is, suffering on account of faithfulness)

The Word

The church has God's Word. It has God's Word in the presence of the risen Christ, the Word Incarnate. The church also has God's Word in the scriptures and in the preached word spoken and heard week in and week out in congregations. "Wherever you hear or see this word preached, believed, professed, and lived," Luther writes, "do not doubt that the true *ecclesia sancta catholica*, 'a Christian holy people,' must be there, even though their number is very small."[3]

Holy Baptism

From its earliest days, the church has practiced baptism as a mark of membership in the body of Christ. Paul can't say for sure who he baptized in Corinth, and his comment about this memory lapse is one of the earliest written testimonies we have to Christian baptism (1 Corinthians 1:14-16). In Matthew 28:16-20, the risen Jesus tells his disciples to go to all nations, making disciples, baptizing them and teaching them to obey what Jesus has commanded. In one of the later Pauline letters, we read, "when the goodness and loving-kindness of God our Savior appeared, he saved us, not because of any works of righteousness that we had done, but according to his mercy, through the water of rebirth and renewal by the Holy Spirit" (Titus 3:4-5).

Holy Communion

The Gospels of Matthew, Mark, and Luke, along with Paul's First Letter to the Corinthians, tell the story of Jesus instituting the Lord's Supper on the night of his arrest. Jesus shared bread and wine with his disciples, saying, "This is my body . . . ; this is my blood." We do this in remembrance of him, as the texts record Jesus himself instructing his disciples to do.

The Forgiveness and Reproof of Sin

In the New Testament, Jesus is accused of blaspheming when he announces the forgiveness of sins to a paralyzed man, Mark 2:1-12. "Who can forgive sins but God alone?" bystanders ask. Jesus responds to their question by healing the man's paralysis (Mark 2:7). Jesus accomplishes the visible physical healing in order to show that he has the authority to announce something unseen but nonetheless dramatic, the forgiveness of sins.

Elsewhere in the Gospels Jesus gives his disciples the authority to forgive sins—the very authority that had been presumed to belong to God alone. After his resurrection, he says to the gathered disciples, "Receive the Holy Spirit. If you forgive the sins of any, they are forgiven them; if you retain the sins of any, they are retained" (John 20:22-23).

The Office of the Ministry

The earliest Christians apparently had certain divisions of labor for the work of ministry and evangelism. Apostles, prophets, deacons, bishops, pastors, and teachers: these are all mentioned in the New Testament, though no set schema of offices is available in the canon or apparently deemed necessary in the earliest church. When Luther lists the office of the ministry among the marks of the church, he is most interested in the work of that office to proclaim the Word of God, to administer Holy Baptism and Holy Communion, and to announce the forgiveness of sins. In other words, those who hold offices of ministry in the church "publicly and privately give, administer, and use the aforementioned four things or holy possessions in behalf of and in the name of the church."[4]

Worship, or Public Prayer

"Sixth," Luther writes, "the holy Christian people are externally recognized by prayer, public praise, and thanksgiving to God." The psalms and the Lord's Prayer are biblical resources for prayer and central to the worship of Christian congregations. In addition, when Luther writes about this mark of the church, he endorses the use of any "prayers and songs which are intelligible and from which we can learn and by means of which we can mend our ways."[5]

The Holy Cross

Finally, the church is recognized by the suffering it endures as a result of following the Crucified One. Jesus' own message encounters opposition that leads finally to his death by crucifixion. Can disciples expect a different reaction than their teacher received (Matthew 10:24-25)? Jesus tells his disciples that because of their association with him, they too will be persecuted. Throughout the history of the church, Christians have borne testimony to the joy that attends the Christian life, but their stories also testify to the opposition they encounter as they seek to follow Jesus in love for God and neighbor.

Martin Luther concludes his remarks on these signs by saying, "These are the true seven principal parts . . . whereby the Holy Spirit effects in us a daily sanctification and vivification in Christ."[6] To *sanctify* something is to make it holy; to *vivify* it is to give it life. These are the means by which the Holy Spirit makes Cristians holy and breathes into us the life of the risen Christ.

Luther's mention here of *daily* sanctification and vivification begs the question of how these marks of the corporate body of Christ, the church, connect with daily life. How does what happens at church give shape and depth to the day-to-day life of those who gather for worship each week? Each of the next seven chapters takes up that question by focusing on one of the signs and considering some of the benefits of participating in a Christian congregation for the way we live from day to day.

For each sign, I have chosen a New Testament story that brings the sign to life. The unnamed woman who anoints Jesus before his death will introduce us to the story where we belong; Zacchaeus will welcome us to the table where we belong, and so on. From there, we will explore what each sign means for the everyday lives of people who participate in it. Jesus proclaimed that the reign of God was at hand, and he demonstrated its nearness in his ministry. I believe the marks of the church are signs of belonging to that reign of God here and now, and I hope to show how it is present in our daily lives.

Questions for discussion

1. Choose one of Luther's marks of the church and describe a time when it has had an impact on your life. What happened, and what did it mean to you?
2. If you attend church regularly, why do you do that? What do you find there? If you do not, what might make it more worthwhile in your life?
3. Imagine you are describing the church to someone who has never been there. Role-play this scene, if volunteers are willing. Someone can be an interested but uninformed seeker. Someone else can try to answer the seeker's questions about what Christians do. What would you ask, if you were the seeker? What would you reply, if you were the church member?

2

The Word: The Story Where We Belong

A friend of mine is thinking of trying "speed-dating." It is something like a card game where your partner changes with every hand. Couples talk to each other for eight minutes, then move to a new partnership. In the course of an evening, one meets ten prospective "dates." At the end of the evening, the proprietor of the dating service collects requests for contact information and distributes phone numbers according to the wishes of both parties.

The whole idea makes my head spin. I'm pretty sure the practice would require a level of concentration I do not have in order to remember ten names, faces, stories, and first impressions in one evening. What interests me about the process is the amount of time chosen for each date. Eight minutes. Think about walking into a strange church: you know a thousand things after eight minutes. If you are there for a worship service, you know whether you can find the place for the service, whether anyone is glad to see you, whether you will like the music, whether anyone is your age, color, or class, and whether that matters for how you will be accepted, whether the flow of the service will be familiar or foreign, and on and on. Eight minutes into a church "date," most of us will have a pretty good idea whether we could ever feel like we belonged in a new place, with the people there.

In Mark 14, Jesus is on the verge of his arrest and death. The story is winding down for him—or heating up, depending on your perspective. In either case, a few days before his death he finds himself in Bethany, just outside Jerusalem, at the home of a man identified as "Simon the leper," Mark 14:3-9. As they are having dinner, something happens. "A woman came with an alabaster jar of very costly ointment of nard, and she broke open the jar and poured the ointment on his head" (Mark 14:3). The woman has appeared out of nowhere. We do not know where she has come from; we never learn her name; other gospel accounts add some detail about her, but here—nothing.

As unidentified as she is, we see enough in the next verse to recognize that she has miscalculated whether she belongs in the house of Simon the leper and whether her actions will be understood or welcomed. People start grumbling. They scold her, saying, "Why was this ointment wasted in this way? It could have been sold for more than three hundred denarii and the money given to the poor" (Mark 14:4-5).

Imagine spending a year's salary on one *big* party at your church. In a matter of minutes—or hours at the most—your money will be gone. As you're tying the last of about a thousand balloons into place, several people walk up to you and say, "We know you mean well, but we just don't think you understand our vision for mission. We are a church that cares passionately about social justice. We want people to have enough to eat. Why on earth would you spend so much money on a party? Apparently frivolous things are more important to you than they should be." It's a great speech for your sense of belonging, right? That is the kind of speech the woman receives from those who see what she gives Jesus.

The bystanders decide she has wasted the ointment. Jesus, however, defends her actions. "She has performed a good service for me," he tells everyone (Mark 14:6). He goes on, "You always have the poor with you, and you can show kindness to them whenever you wish, but you will not always have me." What is the good service that the woman has done? According to Jesus, "She has anointed my body beforehand for its burial. Truly I tell you, wherever the good news is preached in the whole world, what she has done will be told in remembrance of her" (Mark 14:9).

With that, the woman receives a place in the gospel. We still don't know her name, but she is in the story. She belongs. In fact, her work prefigures work that Jesus has yet to do. She makes a generous sacrifice, is mocked in the midst of it, but is vindicated by a force stronger than all that the scoffers have available to them. It is a story that Jesus and the woman share. Sacrifice, greeted by mockery, yet followed by vindication: this is the story that unfolds for Jesus at the cross.

The story of the woman anointing Jesus can help us understand the first sign of belonging, the Word: the story where we belong. Here are some of the elements of that story: (1) it includes Jesus and (2) a mishmash of other people; (3) it intersects significantly with death, and (4) it has global reach.

Jesus as the story's main character

When Martin Luther says that the church is the church because it has the Word, he is speaking as much of the Word made flesh—that is, Jesus—as he is speaking of the proclaimed Word or the Word of the Holy Scriptures. The story where we belong is not just defined by its plot, so that any story of "death and resurrection," would work to tell the truth about us. The story of a flower bulb lying beneath the winter snows, apparently dead but then able to be a daffodil in the spring—it's a good story, and even a true story, but it is not the Christian story. The plot has points of contact with our own, but our story is defined by its character as much as its plot, and its main character is Jesus of Nazareth. Preaching professor Charles Campbell makes this point eloquently in his book, *Preaching Jesus* (Grand Rapids: Eerdmans, 1997). It is Jesus, the rabbi, healer, and exorcist, the one who is about to be killed, who is at table when the woman with the alabaster jar comes into Simon's house. It is in the story of Jesus that we belong.

Some years ago, I was teaching a class on the historical Jesus in Luther Seminary's Lay School of Theology. Week after week, I spoke about how little we can really know about the actual person, Jesus, who lived during the same time as John the Baptist and Pontius Pilate. Even so, the class was full, and people were eager to know what those who study and write on the topic of the historical Jesus really believed. I was skeptical that we could get very far behind the Gospels themselves and back to the real time when Jesus walked around that little patch of land in the Middle East where he lived and worked. After one of the classes, I asked a participant why he was there. What was the appeal of a class about history for which we have extraordinarily limited sources? Mark replied simply, "I want to know Jesus." "Oh," I answered. "Right." I had thought this was all some kind of academic pursuit for my class, and it had not made sense to me at that level. But wanting to know Jesus: that I understood.

Think of all the plot lines that surround us: "Somewhere in the darkest night a candle glows." Or "You don't get what you deserve. You get what you negotiate!" Or "Computers are running our lives." Or "Might makes right." In contrast to these, Christians confess that the true story about our lives is bound up with the story of a 1st century Jew named Jesus and with the God to whom he was and is as close as can be.

A mishmash of other people

Our story also includes lots of other people. There is a leper who is having a dinner party; that in itself is remarkable. The translators of the Contemporary English Version were so astounded by that possibility that they refer to the man as "Simon, who once had leprosy" (American Bible Society, 1995). Closer to the Greek text is the standard translation, "Simon the leper." Simon is hosting a dinner.

Our story also includes that astoundingly bold and generous woman without a name. In ancient Israel, leaders such as prophets, priests, and kings were anointed. *Messiah* (from Hebrew) or *Christ* (from Greek) means "anointed one." In the story of Jesus, when is he ever anointed? He becomes an anointed one here, in this story. The anointing happens by a woman whose name is unrecorded, but whose story is nonetheless yoked to the story of Jesus, his status as Messiah, and his death.

There are grumblers, too, in our story, people who get angry at the show of extravagance and scold the woman for the waste. Recently I visited a friend who had just accepted a call to be pastor of a small church in rural Wisconsin. During a tour of the Sunday school wing, I commented on the murals in almost every room. One wall was covered with small handprints in a rainbow of colors. Another room, with computers in it, had several mice painted on the wall, with pictures of Swiss cheese wedges spaced between them. A third room had been turned into a kind of theater with a little stage at one end and walls that were painted midnight blue. I confess, I was a little disoriented. My friend had told me that this was the education wing, but no light green or noncommittal easy-care beige was in sight. I commented on the wild walls, and Roger replied, "My favorite part of working here is that people can paint the walls without having to get permission from the church council." He was talking about paint—and about a whole lot more than that. Imagine a Sunday school wing where teachers and students could actually paint and repaint the walls, willy-nilly! If you are new to the church, this thought experiment might not seem particularly dramatic to you. If you have been around the church for a while, chances are the prospect of painting walls without getting permission elevates your heart and respiration rates a little. "Someone will complain. Someone will hate it. Someone will say we are wasting time and money. Do we dare? Is it worth the fuss it will cause?" Most of our churches include at least a few people who could play the part of the grumblers in the story of Jesus' anointing. Maybe we are those grumblers sometimes. "Why this waste?" we want to know. "Where will it end?"

Death in the story

Where will it end? Indeed! Jesus says, "You will not always have me." He is talking about his own end. As the woman breaks the jar and pours the nard over Jesus, his own death is almost close enough for him to smell. In a matter of days, he will be really, truly dead. "She has anointed my body beforehand for its burial" (Mark 14:8). It is sweet perfume she pours, and it doubles as embalming fluid. Jesus is not on the verge of pretending to die; he is on the verge of dying.

Religion in general and Christianity in particular has sometimes been characterized as an intricate lie told for the purpose of denying death. A nonreligious friend once explained his rejection of Christianity to me by saying, "Look, I believe that when you're dead, you're dead." Honesty matters a great deal to my friend, and he will not "make believe" about something like that. I wish I had said to him that Christians would agree with him. We also believe that when you're dead, you're dead. Death is so real for us that the apostle Paul calls it "the last enemy to be destroyed," and he tells us what we already know: We hope for the destruction of death, and we trust that it will happen, but it is not something we see yet. Like my nonreligious friend, we know that when you're dead, you're dead. It's just that we do not think God will leave us dead any more than we think that God left Jesus dead. We trust in something we cannot know as clearly as we know the part about death being real. Nonetheless the resurrection is our hope, the certainty of which we believe God has borne witness to by raising Jesus from the dead.

The story's global reach

Finally, the story where we belong is also the story where all sorts of other people belong. In Revelation 7, people of every nation, tribe, people, and language gather around the throne to worship the risen Lord. When Jesus commends the woman's good work for him, he says, "Wherever the good news is preached, in *all the world*, what she has done will be told in remembrance of her" (Mark 14:9). Paul defends his ministry at one point by saying, "This was not done in a corner" (Acts 16:26). From time to time, the church has tried to be small, enclosed, and insular, circling the wagons against dangers present in the "outside world." Always in these times, someone remembers that "God so loved *the world* that he sent his only Son" (John 3:16). The story where we belong is not a possession that can be grasped and guarded. We, and people like us, and people very different from us belong in it.

Having the Word, reading the Scriptures

Those of us who are not as bold as the woman with the jar of ointment may have some anxiety as we consider stepping into the story of Scripture. Do we really belong there? Will we ever know the Bible well enough? What if we make mistakes? What about the parts that are hard to understand? What about the parts we do not like?

Years ago, I heard a woman telling the story of her predominately white church beginning a relationship with a neighboring African American church. The idea was that members of both churches would see each other at occasional picnics and joint worship services and work days. They would start doing service projects and fellowship events together, with the hope that their members would grow in friendship and in understanding for one another. At one of the organizational meetings, a man from the white church, who was particularly anxious about what they were planning, admitted how uncomfortable he was. "I'm just so afraid I'll make a mistake," he said.

"Of course, you will," one of the black men at the table said to him. "We all will."

As we read the Scriptures, we are bound to make mistakes. Sometimes we will read things all wrong. A rereading, a sermon on the text, or a friend who is reading with us will point out something we missed altogether. We will make mistakes. You can misunderstand the Bible, but you can't break it. And imagine how impoverished your life would be if you never made a new friend or received another guest in your home for fear of the misunderstandings that inevitably come when people get to know each other over time. We get to know someone over a series of interactions with them; the relationship has certain features when it is just beginning, and it develops and changes as time goes on. Getting to know the Bible is more like getting to know another person than it is like mastering a skill or finishing a task.

Anyone who has lived in close proximity to other human beings knows what it is like to be angry at or put off by someone you love. All of us who live with the Bible can name parts of it that are—depending on the day and the situation!— very hard to love. What was Paul thinking when he said that women should be silent in the churches (1 Corinthians 14:34-36)? Isn't he actually contradicting what he himself has said elsewhere (see Galatians 6:26-29)? Doesn't it seem peevish and impulsive for God to wipe out all the humans on earth except for Noah and his family (Gen. 6—8)? What was Jesus trying to say about God when he told that story of the vineyard owner who made the workers who had worked a full day watch as he paid the late comers the same wage the all-day workers had received? Wasn't that unfair (Matthew 20:1-16)? There is plenty to be either puzzled or repelled by in these writings.

Barbara Brown Taylor says this of her relationship with the Bible:

> [It] "is not a romance, but a marriage, and one I am willing to work on in all the usual ways: by living with the text day in and day out, but listening to it and talking back to it, by making sure I know what is behind the words it speaks to me and being certain I have heard it properly, by refusing to distance myself from the parts of it I do not like or understand, by letting my love for it show up in the everyday acts of my life."[1]

Like life, the story where we belong comes with parts we do not like or understand.

It may help here to point out that Christians confess that the Bible is God's Word, with human fingerprints all over it. Both things are true about this book. Incarnation is the way God has chosen to be with us; that is, God has taken on flesh and blood in

Jesus of Nazareth. Likewise, God gives us God's own Word, yet God does so by giving us the words of human beings like Moses, Paul, and others. For me, this means that to live with the Bible is sometimes to live, not just with parts of God that are hard for me to love, but with the parts of Paul, or Mark, or Amos that are hard to love. Such is the gift of the Scriptures: to step into this story is to get to know dozens of complicated human beings through whom God speaks. God cares enough about human history to be involved in it, so God's Word is not cut loose from moorings in time and place as it comes to us in the scriptures.

Neither are we disembodied, cut loose from time and place, as we read God's Word. Just like the writers, so also we readers of Scripture bring our history and our hopes to each encounter with the Bible. One of the clearest ways to see how much of ourselves we bring to reading is to read with someone else. Others will see things we missed, maybe even things we never imagined were there. One of the great gifts of the Reformation is the conviction that the Bible can and should be read by all of God's people. Ask friends what they make of a biblical story you are thinking about. Ask a teenager or a child. Ask someone of the opposite sex, or someone of another cultural background. What do they see? The church together receives the Word. Ask others what they have received.

The Bible is for all of God's people, even—I am happy to report—religious professionals. People who write Bible studies, Bible dictionary articles, and notes in modern editions of the Bible are co-readers with the rest of those who receive the Word. Scholars often point out things that show us relationships between one part of the Bible and another, or between a biblical text and its original time and place. Artists and poets get in on the act, too. A hymn, a picture, a sermon on the text—these, too, are ways that other witnesses to the truth of Scripture accompany us as we step into the biblical story.

At this point, it may seem that the party is getting a little loud. Voices from various parts of Scripture, musings of scholars, ideas from your thirteen year-old, a hymn from another century or this one—are we receiving God's Word or experiencing only human cacophony?

The inspiration of the Holy Spirit is the difference between the two. It is commonly known that Christians believe that God inspired the Scripture. The words "inspire" and "spirit" are related. God breathed God's Spirit into the prophets' speaking, the apostles' letter-writing, the evangelists' story-telling. Less commonly known is that Christians also believe and pray that God will inspire the reading of God's Word as much as God inspired the writing of that Word. The Holy Spirit worked through humans to write the Scriptures. The Holy Spirit works through humans who are reading them as well.

When I started reading the Bible in academic settings, I was taught to be ever mindful of the distance between the original audience and my time and place. To collapse the distance between "then" and "now" was to risk misunderstanding the text and seeing in it nothing more than my own self-absorbed and self-referential interpretation. Such a risk is real, of course. As we keep company with the scriptures, there will be times when they rightly seem strange and distant from our experience. If they never seem strange and distant, it is likely that we are not really reading and receiving a word from outside ourselves, but merely creating the scriptures in our own image.

Yet, as risky as it is for all concerned, the overall story of Scripture, as well as the shorter stories within it—like this story of a woman doing such a wild, extravagant, and death-anticipating anointing of Jesus—invite us to step into them and to find the truth about ourselves there. So, for instance, we see in scripture that God did not create just the first humans in God's image. God created *us* in God's image, too. Jesus said to the thief on the cross, "Today you will be with me in paradise" (Luke 23:43), yet his words show us something so profound about his capacity for love of a neighbor that we conclude he could—and does—love not just the thief but us as well. As we read, learn, and make the scriptures our own, the distance between then and now often grows quite small. I worry about this less than I used to. Finally, the story of Jesus, as filled as it is with reversals, grumblers, death, and extravagant devotion, is the story where we belong.

Questions for discussion

1. Read Mark 14:3-9. Is there anything about the story that surprises you? What would you ask Jesus if you were there at the table with him? What would you ask the woman?
2. This chapter offered some cultural stories (computers rule our lives, might makes right, and so forth.) that exist alongside the story of Jesus and vie for our allegiance. Can you think of particular stories you are asked to believe in your daily life? How does that happen in your life? How do those stories compare to what you know about the story of Jesus?
3. Is there a place (school, church, home, work, a favorite trail, somewhere else) where you feel a strong sense of belonging? What is one thing the church could do to offer that sense to more people?

3

Holy Baptism: The Bath Where We Belong

A friend of mine says that she found her way back to the church in young adulthood because she wanted a place like the Cheers bar, "where everybody knows your name," but without the alcohol. She is not alone. In America, such connections have become a selling point for all sorts of things. Health clubs and apartment complexes call themselves communities, and they tell us they are great places to meet and make friends. Internet sites pledge to help us connect with others who share our interests. Telecommunications companies have trendy gadgets with rings, beeps, and reminder alerts to help us stay in touch with those we care about.

The church talks about community at least as much as the rest of the culture does. When we say to someone newly baptized, "We receive you as a fellow member of the body of Christ," we are saying something about our sense of community. We are members of one body.

Fellow members of the body of Christ

In the church, however, we do not base our sense of community on the things that shape community elsewhere: shared interests, tastes, or needs. The basis for community in Christ is *Christ*. In his ministry, Jesus offered forgiveness, healing, and new life to lepers, the slave of a Roman centurion, tax collectors like Matthew and Zacchaeus, children, women, fishermen, and many others who had little in common with each other except for the fact that Jesus was interested in all of them. In the same way, it is Jesus' interest in all of us that binds each of us together with others in the church today.

Is the interest that Jesus has in both you and your neighbor enough glue for a real sense of community? Sometimes it looks to me like those characters on Cheers are having more fun in their community than we ever have at my church. Yet imagine actually living with Cliff or Sam or Carla—would it be any easier than spending time with people who belong to your local congregation? Real life and true community are more complex than even the best TV producers could or would evoke in 30 minutes of programming. To say, "We receive you as a fellow member of the body of Christ," is to say, "Together, we are part of a body that was crucified and raised, and still bears the marks of nails, thorns, and spear. We are in this—living, dying, and rising—together."

The shortest letter of Paul provides a case study for just what that togetherness means for people who try to live it out. Philemon is a one-chapter letter, 25 verses from start to finish, about a page in most Bibles. In some ways it looks like a private letter between the apostle Paul and a businessman named Philemon, so that people might wonder initially what it is doing in the New Testament. Yet the business that Paul needs to transact with Philemon is shaped by the fact that all the principal characters in the letter are members of the body of Christ. The letter is a proclamation of the way baptism into Christ changes even one's business dealings.

Paul begins by addressing the letter "To Philemon our dear friend and coworker, to Apphia our sister, to Archippus our fellow soldier, and to the church that meets in your house" (vv. 1-2). This is a short letter, about one topic that might be seen to concern only Philemon, Paul, and the slave, Onesimus. Yet Paul addresses the letter to everyone. Imagine having an audit report of your company's books read in your congregation on Sunday morning. What is going on here?

From there, Paul pretty much speaks to Philemon directly, using the singular form of "you." Paul is talking to his brother, aware that others are listening in as he does so. Paul begins by remembering and giving thanks for Philemon's faith and his famous hospitality. The hearts of the saints have been refreshed (vv. 4-7).

All good so far. If you were Philemon, however, you might be feeling for your wallet at about this point. And you would be right! Paul's next sentence is this: "For this reason, though I am bold enough in Christ to command you to do your duty, yet I would rather appeal to you on the basis of love—and I, Paul do this as an old man, and now also a prisoner of Christ Jesus" (vv. 8-9). From there, things get a little fuzzy about what exactly Paul wants Philemon to do, but it has to do with Philemon welcoming a slave back into his household, "no longer as a slave but more than a slave, a beloved brother—especially to me but how much more to you, both in the flesh and in the Lord" (v. 16).

Did Onesimus, the slave, run away from Philemon's house? Did he take money from Philemon's accounts? Did he just happen to meet Paul—perhaps in prison—or did he go to Paul seeking intercession between himself and his master? And when did he become a brother in the Lord? Many details are left out of the letter, but it is clear that Paul is appealing to Philemon so that the one who had been Onesimus's master will regard his relationship with Onesimus anew. Onesimus has apparently been baptized, and now Philemon is about to take a bath on certain investments. Baptism is "the bath where we belong" both because it offers forgiveness of sins, effecting a squeaky clean reality for us, and because as a result of baptism, some things in our lives go right down the drain.

Philemon's whole household structure is circling around at the bottom of the tub. Where would a Greco-Roman household be without master-slave relationships? The question is something like asking where democratic capitalism would be without private property, or where the American transportation system would be without automobiles. In a letter that is addressed to "the church that meets in your house," Paul asks Philemon to stop treating this fellow human being as if he were property. If Philemon gets out of the tub and clothes himself with the new human being, Christ (Colossians 3:10; Ephesians 4:24), then he will regard Onesimus no longer as slave, but rather as a brother, and all of the relationships in his household will begin to be reconfigured. It could end in a whole new life.

Children of the same heavenly Father

In the reign of God that Paul is envisioning, all three principal characters in the story—Philemon, Onesimus, and Paul himself— are brothers. They are "children of the same heavenly Father,"[1] as the service of Holy Baptism in *Lutheran Book of Worship* puts it.

Family, of course, is never an uncomplicated reality! In our time, situation comedies make relationships between friends much more appealing than those between family members. The billboard for a mega-mall offers the humorous advice, "Bring your relatives. Then ditch them." Welcome to the *family*?

As Jesus defines it, family offers permanence that other kinds of relationships do not. "The slave does not have a permanent place in the household; the son has a place there forever" (John 7:35).

The words ring true. Even if your family turns out to be not your favorite group to spend time with, they are harder to ditch than the mega-mall's billboard might suggest! Yet Jesus refers to himself as God's son and to his disciples as his brothers (John 20:17). Describing Jesus' work, the evangelist says, "To all who received him, who believed in his name, he gave power to become children of God" (John 1:12). To say, "welcome to the Lord's family," is to say, "Here is a set of relationships, a home, and an inheritance that belong to you—forever."

So, what does it mean to spend your days as part of the Lord's family? Is this way of speaking anything more than the pious language of worship books and hymnals?

In the fall of 2002, Minnesotans lost the state's senior senator, Paul Wellstone, when he was killed in a plane crash along with his wife, their daughter, three campaign workers, and two pilots. Shortly after the tragedy, a banner appeared over the entrance to the building on the University of Minnesota campus where one of the lost campaign aides, Mary McEvoy, had worked. The banner carries a quote from McEvoy: "What would you do if anything were possible and you knew you could not fail?" What would you do? What would you no longer fear? What could you try? What would be the fruit of that kind of freedom?

McEvoy's question evokes a freedom for daily living like that which belongs to those welcomed into the Lord's family. If you knew you could not fail . . . if, for instance, you knew that your needs would be supplied as surely as the lilies of the field and the birds of the air are fed and clothed (Matthew 6:25-34) . . . if you were freed from anxiety about such things, what might you spend that extra energy doing? Or if your place in God's home and family were assured, and you did not have to cajole God—or anyone else—into loving you, what would you do with all that extra time?

In this scenario, life is more like getting to spend your time managing the assets of the family's charitable foundation than it is like working to pay the bills. In your job with the foundation, there are still decisions to be made that require thoughtfulness and care, but you are not operating from *fear* anymore. What would you do if you were welcomed into the Lord's family and you knew your place there was secure?

Workers in the kingdom of God

If Philemon and Onesimus start living as brothers, rather than as master and slave, it does not mean that the work around the house stops getting done. It does mean, however, that that work is done differently. When we welcome the newly baptized into the congregation, we refer to ourselves as *workers together in the kingdom of God*. The phrase points toward two elements of our everyday lives.

In one sense, Christians are together in a congregational life. As a 20-something, bookish, shy "professional" trying hard to act all grown up, I was thrown into a ropes course with members of a senior high youth group. I was not the youth pastor. I don't even remember how I came to be on the trip we were taking. But I remember the ropes course. We had to help each other out of certain orchestrated problems, like climbing out of an enclosure without using any props. It was not a dangerous course, but it did require teamwork, imagination, and shared strength. I fully expected that the most athletic members of the group would turn the experience into a kind of *Survivor* episode and vote people like me (and I was pretty sure I was the only person like me) off the island.

It didn't happen. If the beautiful people thought any of the rest of the group were losers, they did not let on. Our group experienced two hours of interaction without ridicule—something at least as dramatic as Paul's announcement that Philemon and Onesimus are now brothers in Christ. Freshmen and sophomores worked with juniors and seniors to solve the puzzles. People with strong arms made ladders and lifted the weaker members. We worked out the problems that the course presented. Somehow, for that afternoon, even the strongest among us seemed to understand that they were stronger with the rest of us than they were alone. Shared work became a way into actually living the community that is "on paper" when Christians call ourselves members of one body. "We welcome you to the Lord's family." It is a welcome to the work that we will do together.

The second meaning of the phrase has to do with everyday life and work, that is, with what we do at home, at work, in the community—not just at church or with other Christians. Paul prays that Philemon may "perceive all the good that we may do for Christ" (v. 6), as if all sorts of good were possible and what we needed most was a way to see our daily work as work for Christ.

Lutherans speak often of a doctrine of vocation, by which we mean that daily work is holy, not just the work of special vocations, like a calling to church work, for instance. Being a good parent, accountant, musician, poet, or politician is just as much a way to participate in "all the good we may do for Christ" as is any office of ministry. Jesus summarized the law by speaking of love for God and neighbor (Mark 12:31). By working on behalf of the neighbor, we bear witness to the reality that in a world where many would-be rulers vie for our allegiance and fruit of our labor, we are part of *God's* rule. Freedom for such work is one of the gifts of baptism.

Membership in the body of Christ, a permanent place in the household, meaningful work for the neighbor: all these are yours. What would you do if anything were possible and you knew you could not lose these?

Questions for discussion

1. How important to you is it that everyone in your church community knows your name? How connected do you feel to the other member of the "family" of believers? How might you feel or become more connected?

2. Are you baptized? If so, how—if at all—is it important in your life? Does it change anything about how you live? If not, how might Baptism change things in your life?

3. What would you do if anything were possible, and you knew you could not fail?

4

Holy Communion: The Table Where We Belong

In the stories we have about him, Jesus does a lot of eating. He eats with his disciples, with at least one Pharisee, and with his friends Mary, Martha, and Lazarus. Twice he eats in the desert with thousands of people, who share small amounts of food and then find themselves with baskets of leftovers. He eats before his death and after his resurrection. Often he is a guest at someone else's table; at least once he is the cook, offering some tired fishermen breakfast on the beach after a long night's work.

In Luke 19:1-10, Jesus is passing through Jericho. It is the last town he will go through before he arrives in Jerusalem, where he will be killed. As he walks along, he draws the attention of the townspeople, especially someone named Zacchaeus, a chief tax collector and a rich man. Either because Zacchaeus is short, or because Jesus is short (the text is ambiguous in Greek and in most English translations), Zacchaeus cannot see Jesus, so he runs ahead of the parade of people and climbs a tree to see him. When Jesus looks up to find Zacchaeus in the tree, Jesus invites himself to the tax collector's house for dinner. "Hurry and come down; for I must stay at your house today" (v. 5). Zacchaeus hurries down and receives Jesus with joy.

In Jesus' time, chief tax collectors were chief collaborators with Roman imperial oppression. Zacchaeus is a Jew who has become wealthy by collecting money from his own people and passing some of that money on to Rome. He may or may not have been corrupt. He was, however, certainly in a slimy business. So when Jesus goes into the tax collector's home, the people who see it grumble, "He has gone into be the guest of one who is a sinner" (v. 7). The people are right, of course. Jesus has made the decision to be the guest of a sinner. He decides that he belongs at the table of the tax collector, no matter what bystanders will think.

When a friend of mine was in high school, his best friends were kids on the edges—the edge between passing and failing classes, the edge between keeping the rules and breaking them, the edge between staying in school and dropping out. Zachary's mom worried about the company he kept. Didn't he know that "bad company ruins good morals" (1 Corinthians 15:33)? He was a kind, smart kid. Something bad could happen to him in a bad crowd. Yet when she talked with Zach about this, he told her he wanted the influence to run the other direction. He wanted to be a good influence for the others. Might not good company transform bad morals? Zach had thought about this question and was hoping his company would make it possible for his friends to back up from the edge a few steps.

Might not good company transform bad morals? While Jesus is a guest in the home of the tax collector, neither of them talks about the grumblers outside the door. Actually, we do not know what they talked about at all. All we know is that at some point in the visit, the tax collector stands up and makes this speech: "Look, half of my possessions, Lord, I will give to the poor; and if I have defrauded anyone of anything, I will pay back four times as much" (v. 8). Jesus replies, "Today salvation has come to this house, because he too is a son of Abraham. For the Son of Man came to seek out and to save the lost" (vv. 9-10).

The crowd, the rich man running like a boy and climbing a tree, the teacher inviting himself to dinner, the grumblers who know Zacchaeus is a sinner, Zacchaeus's promise to give away half of his possession and make fourfold restitution for fraud, Jesus' announcement that salvation has come to this house today: I'm thinking, "Where is this church? I would like to be a member!" Watching this story unfold is a lot more dramatic than watching members of our congregation file up to the altar rail for a bit of bread and a little wine. Yet the events have at least one thing in common: over and over again at table with the Lord, sinners are transformed.

Jesus makes the decision that he belongs at the table of the tax collector, no matter what bystanders will think. Jesus also decides that people like Zacchaeus—that is, sinners—belong at his table. "The Son of Man came to seek out and to save the lost," he says about his own mission. When we share the Lord's Supper together, we are participating in that mission. We gather around the table of the one Zacchaeus calls, "Lord," and we eat together.

That we eat *together* is a central aspect of this mark of the church. In 1984, Sally Field starred in the movie *Places in the Heart*. In it, she played Edna Spalding, a woman who was trying to hold on to a farm after her sheriff husband had been killed. At the start of the film, in response to that killing, the man who shot her husband is dragged through town behind a hay wagon until he dies. This is our welcome to the world of the film. Most of the film is the story of how a black man by the name of Moze (short for Moses?) helps Edna to keep her farm going and harvest her cotton crop. Members of the Ku Klux Klan harass Edna, burning down her barn when it is full of cotton, and they try to kill Moze. When one of the sheets covering a Klan member's face is torn off during a fight, Edna recognizes the man behind the sheet as one of her neighbors.

The film is full of all the difficulties that human beings face when we try to live as a community. If this is a picture of the communion of saints—and by the end of the film, there is good reason to believe it is—then that communion is deeply flawed.

The story ends with the characters in church. Congregation members are sharing the Lord's Supper. First, we see Edna, and then the camera angle widens to include her son, and widens further to include her husband, who had been killed at the start of the film. There he is, in church, receiving the Lord's Supper. In the next row back, we see the man who killed Edna's husband and was himself killed in response. Not far from him are some of the Klan members. Also in the church, receiving Communion in the pews along with everyone else, is Moze, the man who helped Edna raise and harvest her crop. Black and white people are together in the church. People capable of great measures of good and evil are there. Even living and dead people are there together, restored to one another, sitting side by side, and learning anew to live together.

The close of the film looks something like the close of the age as Christians understand it. If it was odd for people in Jericho to see Jesus and Zacchaeus eating together, it will be at least as odd to see the mix of people gathered at table with the Lord on the last day. Then, the ways we have divided ourselves from each other, whether within the church or beyond it, will no longer be the truth about us.

Even death—that uncompromising divider of humans one from another—will not have the power to separate us from others any longer. In the last century, when churches and cemeteries were built on the same plot of ground, the cemetery was often designed in a semicircle behind the church building, and the altar rail was a semicircle within the sanctuary. Together, the saints below and the graves of the saints above formed an unbroken ring around the Lord's table. The architecture is a testimony to Christians' understanding of the Lord's Supper as a foretaste of the feast to come, when the circle will indeed be unbroken.

All that togetherness is built into this public sign or mark of the church. When I am among those filing up for my little morsel of food at Communion, I rarely think of the breadth of connection I have to others with whom Jesus wants to eat, but it is all there in miniature, in our actions together, and from time to time, I am blessed with a sense of how much bigger this communion is than what a single pair of myopic eyes can see.

The connections in the Lord's Supper are not just horizontal, of course, but also vertical. That is, the bridges built are not just between us and other humans but also between us and God.

As Matthew tells the story of Easter morning (Matthew 28:1-15), an earthquake and an angel are together responsible for the stone being rolled away from the tomb where the body of Jesus had been laid. In response to the earthquake, and to the appearance of an angel who looks like lightning, everyone in the security detail guarding the tomb faints dead away from fright. Mary Magdalene and the other Mary do manage to maintain consciousness, and to them, the angel says, "Do not be afraid. I know that you are looking for Jesus who was crucified. He is not here; for he has been raised, as he said. Come, see the place where he lay. Then go quickly and tell his disciples, 'He has been raised from the dead, and indeed he is going ahead of you to Galilee; there you will see him.' This is my message for you" (Matthew 28:5-7).

The women take to heart everything that the angel says, except for that part about not being afraid. Matthew says they leave the tomb with fear and great joy. They are joyful, but it does not appear that they feel exactly safe. They are living in a world where the ground is not staying put under their feet, and where at least one of the dead is reported to have not stayed dead. Neither of these realities would inspire a feeling of security. Both frightened and joyful, the women run to tell the disciples. On the way, they run into Jesus. Jesus, like the angel before him, says to the women, "Do not be afraid" (v. 10).

"Do not be afraid." This time the sentence as it is spoken by Jesus has the desired effect. It is the last time fear is mentioned in the Gospel.

Years ago, as someone poured wine from a chalice into my communion glass, he said, "The blood of Christ, shed *for* you." It was a jarring emphasis on the preposition. Readers and liturgists know that prepositions are not the most important words in a sentence. The line is usually spoken, "The blood of Christ shed for *you*," and it probably should be spoken that way. But that day, when the assisting minister punched the preposition, I thought, for the first time in my life, "You know, it could have gone the other way. The blood of Christ could have been shed *against* me."

When Jesus says, "Do not be afraid," he makes it clear that what could have happened did not. The earthquake and the resurrection are both ancient signs that the end is at hand. But what kind of end? Until the women see Jesus, they do not know precisely what kind of end it will be. What about those who deserted Jesus, and the one who denied him, and those who were powerless to do anything but look on as the grisly scene of crucifixion unfolded? What about them? What about us who have been enemies of the good and lived apart from what God wants for us? In the end, will we all find that his blood is a judgment *against* us? "Do not be afraid," Jesus says. "Go and tell my brothers to go to Galilee; there they will see me" (v. 10). The Sacrament of the Altar is for us, not against us. It is the public sign of God's work in Christ to reconcile the world to himself.

Finally, in addition to offering a sign of Christian community as it will be in the resurrection, and a sign of our having been reconciled to God in Christ *today* (as salvation had come to the house of Zacchaeus "today"), the practice of Holy Communion also offers us everyday moments of divisions overcome.

In her novel *Evensong*, Gail Godwin writes the story of an Episcopal clergy couple. One night as they are getting ready for bed, Margaret and Adrian have an argument that deteriorates into a series of hurtful misunderstandings. Margaret, who narrates the story, comments that she knew she should stop talking much sooner than she did, but she could not. In the conversation, both people say things they regret.

The next day, Margaret has a funeral to conduct and before the service, Adrian surprisingly appears in the sacristy.

"I've come to assist the priest with the funeral mass." He was carrying his alb over his arm.

"Well thank you," I said. "Even though she could have managed alone."

"Don't I know that. But she's not alone."[1]

The following day, one of Margaret's friends talks with her about the funeral liturgy.

"Watching you and Adrian bowing to each other up at the altar during the communion yesterday was so strange."

"In what way?"

"Well, it was very moving. It was like some graceful little ceremony of mutual regard."

"We were trained by the same Eucharistic teacher at General Seminary. He told us we should always comport ourselves at the altar like creatures showing good manners before their creator."

"No, but the way you bowed to *each other*. Every time he handed you something, or you handed something back to him. I know that was part of the Church ritual, too, but I was lying awake last night thinking about it in a different way. I was thinking, maybe couples ought to have little rituals like that, where they bow to each other. Maybe once at the beginning of the day and once at the end. Maybe at other times, too. As a way of acknowledging to each other—oh, I don't know, that there really is a sacred aspect of what they're trying to do with each other."

I'll take that home to Adrian, I thought: he'll like it as much as I do. I thought: perhaps we've both exhausted our stockpiles of umbrage over that wretched music video and can bend from the waist and get on with what we are trying to do with each other."[2]

(From EVENSONG by Gail Godwin, copyright © 1999 by Gail Godwin. Used by permission of Ballantine Books, a division of Random House, Inc.)

To my knowledge, this benefit does not make it into any of the catechetical lists of the benefits of Holy Communion. Yet I have seen the Holy Communion liturgy become a time when grumpy Christians behave toward each other better than we would likely be able to behave without the script that is our liturgy.

For instance, from time to time in Communion services, I have been only arm's length from someone I would not have chosen to shake hands with if we were not more or less required to do so by the hymnal. There we are, near each other when the minister says, cheerfully, "Let us share the peace of the Lord with one another." At least one of us groans inwardly. "Peace be with you," we say to each other, mumbling maybe, but the words are out of our mouths, echoing in our common air space. We didn't say them with our fingers crossed. At such a moment, we might imagine what it would be like to have that peace, to share it with others at home, or in the place where we work together. I have known people who sat on opposite sides of the church to avoid encounters like this one with people to whom they could not imagine being reconciled. I have wondered what might happen for them if they just happened to end up near each other one Sunday, and had to act out the script of reconciliation written for them. Might the actions and the public sign of the church within which those actions are set give them a vision of something they could not see before? The table where we belong—the table in our sanctuary—could come to be the setting for a story as dramatic as the one that unfolded around the table that belonged to Zacchaeus.

Questions for discussion

1. Jesus spent much time with notorious sinners like Zacchaeus even though it damaged his credibility with many. Why do you think he did this?

2. Does your faith influence the way you do business, or the way you handle money? If so, how? If not, how do you keep the two separate?

3. Many people experience Holy Communion as a sort of "empty ritual." If it is a meaningful experience to you, how would you describe your experience to someone else?

5

Forgiveness and Reproof of Sin: The Truth Where We Belong

You will know the truth, and the truth will make you free.

☞ *John 8:32*

On the evening of the first day of the week, a couple of days after Jesus had been crucified, the disciples were laying low, playing it safe, shut away behind locked doors. The people who had taken Jesus into custody a few nights before could be coming for them next. They were afraid.

☞ *John 20:19*

Of course, staying inside with the doors locked can get stuffy. Staying anywhere and refusing to budge can be almost suffocating after a while, especially when one is shut in because of fear. I look at the disciples shut up in that room, and I want to say to them, "Can you breathe in there?" There is the beginning of the Christian church, collectively holding its breath in fear, sure that at any moment there will be a knock at the door.

Maybe that's why Jesus doesn't knock. Instead, he just appears in the room with them. There he is, alive, standing among them. And when he appears, he does not say what you might expect: "So where were you when I needed you?" Instead, he says, "Peace be with you," and he shows them his hands and his side. The risen body of Jesus bears the wounds of the crucifixion, proof that God did not just roll back time to raise Jesus from the dead, but instead brought him through death to life again. Jesus greets the disciples and shows them his wounds, and then he says and does something else:

Jesus said to them again, "Peace be with you. As the Father has sent me, so I send you." When he had said this, he breathed on them and said to them, "Receive the Holy Spirit. If you forgive the sins of any, they are forgiven them; if you retain the sins of any, they are retained." John 20:21-23.

With that, the risen Jesus resuscitates a little band of his disciples who had been nearly too scared even to breathe. In liturgy, Lutherans refer to the Holy Spirit as, "the Spirit of our Lord and of his resurrection."[1] In this passage from the Gospel of John, the capacity for disciples to breathe words of rebuke and forgiveness comes from the Holy Spirit breathed into the church by the risen Jesus himself. "You will know the truth, and the truth will make you free," Jesus had said earlier (John 8:32). Giving the disciples the Holy Spirit and empowering them to tell the truth about sin and God's forgiveness of sin—these are among the first things Jesus does to free his friends from that stifling, locked room.

The church has not done so well either in understanding this commission from Jesus or in practicing it. Words of confession and forgiveness are in our worship services, but for many people the words do not come to life there. Strangers to Lutheran liturgy tell old timers that it all sounds rote and formulaic. And outside of church, when personal relationships require telling a hard truth to someone or hearing such a word ourselves, or when we need to give or receive forgiveness within a relationship that is damaged by sin, we are often left to fend for ourselves. What, then, is this mark of the church, and what would it mean for such a mark to be made on our everyday lives?

Maybe we can find our way to a definition of forgiveness by saying first what it is not. Forgiveness of sin is not excusing sin, minimizing it, "reframing" it with another name, or simply ignoring it.

In *All Is Forgiven*, Marcia Witten has analyzed sermons in order to tell how American Protestantism has responded to modern secular culture. She studied dozens of sermons preached in the United States in the late 1980s, all of which were based on the parable of the prodigal son (Luke 15:11-32). The sermons do not respond to sin by naming it and then announcing either its forgiveness or retention. Instead, they do what most of us do most of the time with respect to sin. The sermons bear witness to various methods used by preachers to excuse or ignore sin, whether in the story or in the congregation. As Witten puts it, "the sermons use an impressive array of creative rhetorical devices to deflect the force of notions of sinfulness from 'zinging home' (as one preacher puts it) to their audiences."[2] The message of the sermons is much more like, "God loves us every one," than a direct address to congregation members, "You have sinned," or even the less accusatory word, "We are sinners."

When the prodigal returns home, he says, "Father, I have sinned against heaven and before you" (Luke 15:21). We do not know exactly what the son refers to when he speaks of sin. Is he talking about the way he told his father that he might as well be dead? "Father, give me the share of the property that will belong to me"(Luke 15:12) he had said, asking to fast forward to a division of the estate before his father had even died. Is the son talking about his own bad stewardship of the inheritance, since he "squandered his property in dissolute living" (Luke 15:13)? Or is the sin against heaven the dissolute living itself? The answer is probably all of the above, and more. There are lots of actions in the story that "fall short of the glory of God," as the apostle Paul describes sin (cf. Romans 3:23). Paul says it is the truth about all of us. Sin is everything that drives a wedge between us and other people and between us and God. The 20th-century theologian

Paul Tillich referred to sin as separation, or brokenness. A connection—a relationship—is broken. We are estranged from one another, each diminished by the break. Things are not right. It is fitting that the prodigal son is in "a far country" when he realizes what a hash he has made of things. The reference to place mirrors his spiritual geography.

Imagine that you are on the way to a friend's home for dinner. You get lost and stop to phone for directions. When your friend answers the phone, you describe where you are: "I'm at the intersection of Fourth Avenue and Oak Street," you say, looking at the street signs. It doesn't do a lot of good at this point for your friend to dispute your location with you: "You can't be at that intersection! It's miles from my house!" Unless someone has been toying with the street signs, you probably are where you appear to be, and if your friend doesn't recover from the shock and direct you as if you really were where you apparently are, chances are good that the two of you will miss having dinner together.

In the same way, when sin has broken a relationship, we are farther along the way to reunion when we can speak honestly about the great distance that exists between us and the other than when we stop at merely excusing—that is, making excuses for—sin or ignoring it altogether. It often feels as if we are helping when we say nothing to someone who has hurt us, or when we say, "Oh, don't worry about it; it was nothing really." This keeps us from appearing to be weak or easily bruised by the other. We may even think we are doing the Christian thing, kindly helping the offender not to feel bad since our silence or our minimizing words keep the sin from "zinging home." But when we merely excuse sin rather than addressing it with either rebuke or forgiveness, we are not telling the truth. We are trusting a lie to protect us, and lies cannot overcome the separation of sin. In fact, lies are the best way to drive a wedge between ourselves and another. Ignoring sin, making excuses for it, refusing to use the "s" word to describe it: these all have the effect of trying to place someone at an intersection different from the one where they really are, and then offering them directions. Such a practice makes it nearly impossible ever to sit down to dinner together, reconciled.

In Genesis, Joseph's brothers sell him into slavery, then bloody his clothes with goat's blood and allow their father to believe that his favorite son has been torn apart by wild beasts. Nice guys, these brothers, even if the story makes it clear that Joseph, for his part, was a particularly spoiled and tiresome little brat. While Jacob grieves his beloved son, the young Joseph's life goes from bad to worse. As a slave, his master's wife first tries to seduce him; then, when he refuses her advances, she falsely accuses him of trying to sexually assault her. He is thrown into prison. Eventually, the jailer learns that Joseph can interpret dreams, and things start to turn around for him. The jailer brings him to the attention of the Pharaoh, the king of Egypt, who has been having dreams no one can understand. Joseph interprets the dreams, which predict years of plenty followed by years of famine, and because he has understood the dreams, the Pharaoh places him in charge of grain supplies during the good years so there will be enough stored away for the drought years.

Decades after they sold him into slavery and broke their father's heart, Joseph's brothers come to Egypt looking for grain during the very famine that the Pharaoh had dreamed about (Genesis 42). Joseph provides grain for the brothers, and eventually tells them who he is and brings his family to Egypt to live. Sometime after the reunion, their father dies, and the brothers realize that there is now nothing to stop Joseph from seeking revenge for that little boyish prank of theirs. They go to him, asking for forgiveness.

When the brothers seek forgiveness from him, Joseph does not say, "It's okay, guys. We were all a lot younger then," or, "You know, I guess I was kind of hard to live with." Instead he says, "Fear not, for am I in the place of God? As for you, you meant evil against me; but God meant it for good, to bring it about that many people should be kept alive, as they are today" (Genesis 50:19-20, RSV). With this word, Joseph acknowledges that the brothers meant harm, and he also declares that evil does not have the last word. God's power is greater even than the formidable power of sin, and God has chosen neither to abandon Joseph nor to smite his brothers, but rather to save many people as a result of the brothers' harmful actions. Joseph asks, "Am I in the place of God?" Should Joseph take revenge when God's work through these decades had been to save rather than exact punishment for the offense? Joseph does not second guess God's judgment; he forgives his brothers.

To forgive does not mean to ignore sin or make excuses for it. Instead, to forgive is to decree that sin—that is, something real, damaging, and separation-effecting—does not and will not have the power to dictate the future of relationships it has harmed. In *Traveling Mercies* Anne Lamott asks, "Who was it who said that forgiveness is giving up all hope of having had a different past?"[3] Surely it is that, but forgiveness is not only about the past. It is also a statement of faith about the future. To forgive is to say that the past, which shows no signs of changing, is not the only thing that will determine the shape of the future. "You meant it for evil, but God meant it for good," Joseph tells his brothers. "Receive the Holy Spirit," Jesus says to the disciples. Something intervenes between the past and the future, something that breaks our steady, predictable progress from a painful past into a broken, destructive future. That something is the presence of God, which Jesus calls the Holy Spirit. God intervenes, not to undo the past (remember those scars on the body of the risen Jesus), but to bring about a future that our past would never have let us hope for. "If you forgive the sins of any," Jesus said to his disciples, "they are forgiven them."

There is another statement in the commission Jesus gives his followers. "If you retain the sins of any, they are retained." This is curious. Is the church in the business of binding people's sins onto them for eternity? What is Jesus talking about? Some people will think of other words of Jesus that contrast with the standard interpretation of "retaining sins." For instance, in the Sermon on the Mount, Jesus says, "Do not judge, so that you may not be judged. For with the judgment you make you will be judged, and the measure you give will be the measure you get" (Matthew 7:1-2). And when he encounters a crowd of people about to execute a woman who has been caught in adultery, Jesus says, "Let anyone among you who is without sin be the first to throw a stone at her" (John 8:7). From these verses, it is clear that in that room with his disciples on Easter evening, the risen Jesus must have had something in mind other than the judgment by the righteous against the wicked.

It might help to think about whether in the Gospels Jesus himself ever retains anyone's sin. In several stories, Jesus forgives sin. Does he ever announce the opposite?

Although Jesus forgives sin far more often than he retains it, at least once in the Gospel of John, Jesus speaks words declaring that sin is retained. In John's Gospel, sin is the failure to recognize that Jesus has come from God and is making God known to all the world. In Chapter 9, the sin is the blindness of the religious leaders who believe Jesus must himself be a sinner because he has healed a man on the Sabbath. The leaders do not—they cannot— see that Jesus has come from God and is doing the works of the One who sent him, and so Jesus says to them, "If you were [physically] blind, you would not have sin. But now that you say, 'We see,' your sin remains" (John 9:41). Sin in this context is not moral transgression, but rather the failure to see Jesus for who he is. Sin is the preference to sit in darkness rather than to Jesus, the light of the world (John 3:19, 8:12, 9:5).

At my childhood congregation, in preparation for Holy Communion, the pastor led the congregation in a confession of sin, spoken by all in unison, after which, by the authority of Christ, he declared to all who did "truly repent and believe" in Christ, "the entire forgiveness of all your sins." Then the pastor spoke this second paragraph from our hymnal: "On the other hand, and by the same authority, I declare unto the impenitent and unbelieving, that so long as they continue in their impenitence, God hath not forgiven their sins, and will assuredly visit their iniquities upon them, if they turn not from their evil ways, and come to true repentance and faith in Christ, ere the day of grace be ended."[4] Then, as if the hymnal editors knew that these words might leave us "standin' in the need of prayer," the hymnal directed us to pray together the Lord's Prayer.

These words are the only ones I have ever heard used to carry out the second half of Jesus' commission to his followers, "If you retain the sins of any, they are retained." Other churches have other traditions, including traditions of publicly humiliating those whose sins are the most noticeable, presumably in the hope of inspiring amendment of life, and of providing a frightening disincentive to others who might be considering committing or persisting in similar sins.

I find that old paragraph from the *Service Book and Hymnal*, followed by the prayer to "forgive us our trespasses, as we forgive those who trespass against us" closer to the spirit of Jesus' words to his little church on Easter evening than any practice that effectively pummels sinners with stones of rebuke. When announcing that forgiveness has not happened in certain cases, the minister speaks of impenitence and unbelief. These are not the sins one usually thinks of as requiring rebuke from others, but the speech fits with what we know from John's Gospel. The Pharisees whom Jesus rebukes in John 9 were presumably no worse morally than others of their day; in fact, most of them were likely above average in terms of keeping the rules of their religion. They were pious people, but they persisted in unbelief, even in the face of miraculous signs that pointed to the fact that it was *God* who was working in the works of Jesus of Nazareth. The Pharisees were unbelieving, and they were impenitent, or unyielding, in their unbelief. The result was tragic for them, as it is for all of us when we persist in the false conviction that nothing can break our steady, predictable progress from a painful past into a broken, destructive future. The Pharisees saw no presence of God in the work Jesus did. They were missing God's intervention to bring about a future that the past would never have let them hope for, and so forgiveness—God's very intervention in the present for the purpose of rewriting the future—was lost to them.

This is the risk for all of us. Where are we missing something that *God* is doing, preferring instead to fear, love, and trust in our own luck, or strength, or wits, or to trust in nothing and just resign ourselves to hopelessness? Can anything jar us out of such persistent unbelief?

The hope in Jesus' word about retaining sins is that a word of rebuke from a trusted source, "Look what you're missing!" will have the effect of shaking us awake. Our brothers and sisters in Christ carry out Christ's word when they accurately discern and announce to us that our present path leads to death. Just as "friends don't let friends drive drunk," so Christians do not let brothers and sisters languish in the conviction that we have only ourselves to depend on, or in some other manifestation of unbelief.

Yet how can we really talk to each other about such things? Most polite Christians have little practice even talking about sin, let alone rebuking it! Some generalizations about such talk may help here. First, the rebuke of sin will be clear without being self-right-eous. Remember the Pharisee who catalogued his righteousness in the form of a prayer of thanksgiving? "God, I thank you that I am not like other people: thieves, rogues, adulterers, or even like this tax collector" (Luke 18:11). Jesus did not commend the morally upstanding Pharisee, but in fact declared that the tax collector rather than the law-abiding Pharisee went home justified. Self-righteousness is its own form of fearing, loving, and trusting in one's own wits.

Secondly, a word that rebukes sin will be spoken in humility, since we know that accurately discerning where another is headed may be as hard for us as it was for the Pharisees to see where God was headed when they looked at Jesus. We could be all wrong. Yet the fact that we may be wrong in our estimate of the danger from sin to another's life—and the danger to their immortal soul—does not absolve us of the responsibility to care for one another, and to try to discern danger where danger exists. The fact that we may be wrong means only that whatever we speak, we speak humbly, with as much willingness to listen as to speak. We could, after all, be wrong.

Finally, speaking about another's sin is always in the service of something greater than the rebuke itself. Forgiveness points beyond itself to a future shaped by God's will for abundant life rather than a future shaped by a broken, wounding past. Reproof of sin, just like forgiveness, points beyond itself, aiming ultimately for amendment of life and the renewal of community that has been broken by sin. Whether it is to proclaim forgiveness or to warn of the retention of sins, whenever we speak the "s" word, it is to locate a lost one accurately so that directions home may be offered and we may finally sit down to dinner together. If we do not want to sit at table with those to whom we would offer a word of reproof, we should probably be quiet. Those who receive the reproof may take it to heart, like the Ninevites who annoyed the prophet Jonah terribly when they took him at his word! We could be as successful as Jonah. Then where would we be? Where we will be, in fact, is on the way to a future that the past alone would never have led us to expect.

Questions for discussion

1. If your congregation practices something like the Brief Order for Confession and Forgiveness in *LBW* (p. 56), how do you experience it? Is it meaningful, "just words," or something else?

2. What do you think of the difference drawn here between excusing sin and forgiving it? Is there such a difference?

3. Imagine yourself on the receiving end of either forgiveness or rebuke of sin. Who in your life could tell you such a truth? How would the experience feel?

6

The Office of the Ministry: The Care Where We Belong

So far, we have looked at four signs of the church: the Word, (chap. 2), the Sacraments of Holy Baptism (3) and Holy Communion (4), and the Forgiveness and reproof of sin (5). The fifth sign that Martin Luther mentions is the fact that the church calls and sets apart ministers. Why ministers? Someone needs to pay attention to whether and how the church is actually doing the other practices that constitute it. Is the Word being proclaimed? Is the forgiveness of sins being announced? Are Baptism and Holy Communion being rightly administered? In Lutheran tradition, ministry is as ministry *does*. That is, the church has clergy to ensure that certain things—preaching, administering the sacraments, and proclaiming the forgiveness of sins—are done consistently, publicly, and in good order.

So if ministry is as ministry does, what do ministers *do*, precisely? Most pastors have heard people joke about clergy working only one day a week. Is there more to it than that?

All of the Gospels include the story of Jesus feeding a multitude of people with just a little food. In Mark 6, this feeding happens just after the 12 apostles have returned from a mission trip. They have had success in preaching and healing people (Mark 6:12-13), and they return to Jesus to tell him about their work. After listening to them, Jesus encourages them to "come away to a deserted place all by yourselves and rest a while" (Mark 6:31). Jesus and the disciples attempt to withdraw from the crowds by boat, but the people see where they were going and hurry around the lake on foot, so that when the boat comes to the opposite shore, the disciples are greeted by a great crowd. Not what they had planned.

Even so, Jesus has compassion on the crowds and begins to talk to them. When it grows late, the disciples conclude that it is time for the day's lesson to come to a close. They say to Jesus, "This is a deserted place, and the hour is now very late; send them away so that they may go into the surrounding country and villages and buy something for themselves to eat" (Mark 6:35-36). It is as if the disciples advise Jesus to dismiss the people with a blessing: "Go in peace; keep warm and eat your fill (James 2:16)." But Jesus doesn't do that. Instead, he says to the disciples, "You give them something to eat" (Mark 6:37).

Their eyebrows go up. What? There must be five thousand people here, in the middle of the desert! "Are we to go and buy two hundred denarii worth of bread, and give it to them to eat?" (Mark 6:37). Does Jesus expect them to spend eight months' wages on a picnic? The disciples see the need—so many people are hungry—but they also see clearly their incapacity to meet that need.

Jesus sees things differently. He advises them to take stock of their resources. The disciples come back with the report that they have five loaves and two fish. Jesus tells the disciples to have the people sit down. Then, "taking the five loaves and the two fish, Jesus looked up to heaven, and blessed and broke the loaves, and gave them to his disciples to set before the people; and he divided the two fish among them all. And all ate and were filled; and they took up twelve baskets full of broken pieces and of the fish" (Mark 6:41-42).

"You give them something to eat," Jesus had said. It is a good way of understanding the office of the ministry. The metaphor points not just to the hospitality of a meal shared along the way, but to the activity that makes life possible. Ministry, as it is directed and blessed by Jesus, is the difference between eating and starving. In an essay called "Resurrection and Rhetoric," Richard Lischer lists several reasons for attempting to articulate a theology of preaching that has the cross and resurrection of Jesus at its center. He writes, "How to put it delicately? People are dying . . . We are dying of hate as well as cancer. We are dying of despair as well as disease. But make no mistake about the 'dying' part. Preaching owes those who are dying a word of life."[1]

In John 6, Jesus refers to himself as the bread of life. As they preach, offer spiritual care, and provide the sacraments, ministers of the Word serve up that living bread. However, they do not do it alone. My aim in this chapter is to consider how all of us who participate in a congregation's life share in these three elements of public ministry: preaching, soul care, and administration of the sacraments.

Preaching

When I was a child, it was the custom at our Sunday dinner table to talk about the sermon we had heard at church that morning. My dad, who was not a preacher, was an astute listener, and he always had opinions about what had been preached. We kids were quizzed about what the preacher had said and whether we agreed with it. I don't know whether Dad held these little post-worship debriefings with our family as a way to school his children in the faith, or just because he wanted to talk about what he had heard. Probably both things were going on. In any case, he taught me to listen to sermons as if they mattered, and to think about whether what I was hearing rang true. I was an adult before I realized that not everyone who listens to a sermon talks about it afterward!

This experience also taught me that paying attention to sermons can help make them better. I know this sounds strange, but look back at the feeding miracle. The disciples brought five loaves and two fish to Jesus. As he blessed them, broke them, and gave the pieces back to the Twelve to give to the crowds, there was more than enough food for 5000 people. It is clear in the story that the blessing of Jesus *changes* the meager resources of the disciples. With respect to the proclamation of the Word, the thoughts and comments of nonpreachers can be the means through which Jesus blesses the meager resources of those who preach.

One of the most consistently good preachers I know was the pastor of the church I attended while I was in graduate school. Paul had only been ordained for about three years when I started attending Abiding Savior. He preached without notes, a practice about which I was deeply suspicious. My experience with no-note preachers was that they were often also no-idea preachers. Yet Paul had something to say. Since he had been preaching for only a few years, I figured that his preaching was the result of natural talent. I expected that he had been one of those students in seminary who ace their preaching classes. When I mentioned this to him, he told me that the opposite was true. He had once had to stop and start a sermon over again in preaching lab when the teacher interrupted to ask him, "Do you have everything you need up there?" Paul went back to his backpack to retrieve the manuscript he was supposed to be working without. He also told me about returning to his internship parish a few years after beginning to serve Abiding Savior.

A member of the congregation where he had been a student pastor commented on the change that had happened, saying, "Somebody taught you how to preach."

Paul says that it was the people of Abiding Savior who taught him how to preach. How did they do it? They listened to what he was trying to say, and they talked back to him. Sometimes they talked back to him during the sermon; in fact, if church was too quiet while he preached, that was a way of telling him something, too! Other times, they talked to their preacher after church, or in the middle of the week, or weeks later about something he had said in a sermon.

I have met people who are offended by the thought that sermons may inspire comments. The piety with which they have been raised says that the sermon is God's word to the listeners, and the listeners have no business talking back to God. I appreciate the high regard for the preached word, but the conclusion does not follow from the premise here. Yes, the sermon is God's word, but that doesn't mean that any comment is disallowed. In the scriptures, people talk back to God all the time—each of the psalms is a way of saying, "Listen, Lord, for your servant speaks." In the New Testament, when Ananias hears from the Lord Jesus that he should go and baptize Saul, who has been persecuting the followers of Jesus, Ananias says to the Lord, "Have you thought this through?" or words to that effect (Acts 9:13-14).

Years ago, I was assigned to visit a fourth grader who wanted to quit the confirmation program that had barely begun for him. He was hurt and angry that he had been roped into a program at church that seemed like it would take forever! He wanted out. His mom told me later that before I arrived at the house, she had instructed her son, "You may say anything you want to the pastor, as long as you are not rude." Backtalk—as long as it was polite—was fine. This is how confirmation programs and sermons get better. In practices like listening and talking back, Jesus blesses limited resources. As we speak honestly with our preachers, sermons get more connected to precisely where and how we are "dying of despair as well as disease," and their word of life is more likely to be a word on target for our lives.

Soul care

A friend with roots in the Swedish Covenant church tells me that members of his church have traditionally asked one another, "How is your walk?" It is a deeper question than the greeting, "How are you?" It is asking about one's spirit as well as one's day. How is it being a Christian where you live, where you work? How is it to follow Jesus these days? "How is your walk?" is a soul care question. Soul care is part of the public ministry of clergy, but it is really the work of the whole church; it is listening, speaking, praying, and accompanying. Often people who are not pastors are better at it than the so-called professionals. I have been a hospital patient exactly once in my life, and during that stay I feigned sleep when the strange chaplain stopped by, but I was greatly pleased to see my friends from church. Together they were the "two or three" gathered in Christ's name with me where Christ himself was also present (Matthew 18:20).

Curiously, asking "How is your walk?" changes the very thing about which we ask. The question—if we are serious about it—requires that we fall in beside our conversation partners on the road while we wait for an answer. However their walk is, for the moment at least, they are not alone on it. How is your walk? "Well, maybe not as solitary as it was a moment ago." In *The Noonday Demon*, Andrew Solomon writes about clinical depression, saying,

"So many people have asked me what to do for depressed friends or relatives, and my answer is actually simple: blunt their isolation. Do it with cups of tea or with long talks or by sitting in a room nearby and staying silent or in whatever way suits the circumstances, but do that. And do it willingly."[2] Soul care is walking with someone, blunting the isolation in whatever circumstances, especially in difficult circumstances. It is accompanying that embodies the reconciliation between God and humans that has been won in Christ.

Sacraments

Finally, the office of the ministry exists so that people may receive the sacraments "in good order." When Martin Luther writes about this, he sounds a little worried that things would get out of hand if everyone were allowed to "speak or administer, and no one wanted to give way to the other."[3] It is as if 16th-century churches might soon have the problems of Paul's churches in 1st-century Corinth, where people were all talking at once in worship and the Lord's Supper had become an occasion during which some got drunk and others went away hungry (1 Corinthians 11:17-34). "We need some rules around here," Luther seems to be saying.

Although I am less worried about everyone talking at once than my brother Martin seems to be, I agree that ministers pay attention to things so that the sacraments are neither neglected nor trivialized. I was once a guest at an evening Communion service where the woman who handed me the cup of the Lord's Supper said, "Be nurtured; be nurturing" rather than, "The blood of Christ, shed for you." I was puzzled by the double exhortation. Be nurtured; be nurturing? When I asked her after the service why she said that, she replied, "At first I said, 'The blood of Christ . . . , a few times to people, but then, I don't know . . . . I just didn't like all that talk about blood, so I made up the nurturing sentence."

Years after that experience, it occurred to me that the public office of the ministry exists to ask questions about improvisations like the nurtured/nurturing line. The presiding minister asks, "What are we doing? What are we saying with our words and actions? What is lost in our celebration of the Lord's Supper when we stop using words that Jesus himself used on the night in which he was betrayed?" Anyone in the church can ask those questions, and everyone—whether ordained or lay—should participate in a conversation about them, yet it is part of the work of public ministers to make sure the questions are raised.

Beyond that, the ministers simply "administer." They bear the towels at Baptism. They are wait staff at Holy Communion, as in the story of the feeding. "Hi, my name is Simon Peter and I'll be your server today." The host is Jesus, blessing and breaking bread. He hands the provisions to the disciples, who probably shrug and shake their heads on their way to give the crowds something to eat. Somehow there is more than enough.

Questions for discussion

1. What sorts of things might people in your congregation do to help your preachers preach better? Prayer? Study? Conversation? How could you be involved?
2. Do you know any young people who might be well-suited to the office of the ministry? How might you speak to them about your impression?
3. Have you yourself thought about a call to ministry? Who might be helpful to you or to others who are considering such a call?

7

Worship: The Song Where We Belong

In the seventh chapter of the book of Revelation, John records a vision of a great multitude of people—"too many to count," he says—from every nation, tribe, people, and language. They are standing before the throne of Christ, and they are singing:

> Blessing and honor and glory and pow'r,
> Wisdom and riches and strength evermore,
> Offer to him who our battle has won,
> Whose are the kingdom, the crown, and the throne;
> Whose are the kingdom, the crown, and the throne![1]

The church has a long history of singing this and other scenes from John's vision of that time and place where finally God will wipe away every tear (Revelation 7:17; 21:3-4; cf. Isaiah 25:8) and God's people will be lost in "wonder, love and praise."[2] One of the marks of the church is that it joins in that song ahead of time, here and now, giving voice not only to wonder, love, and praise, but also to need, lament, and thanksgiving. When we engage in public prayer, we are "doing Revelation," as my colleague Craig Koester says. The vision of John comes true as we join in song with brothers and sisters in Christ across the centuries and around the globe. Together we are that multitude around the throne; we are that "Christian holy people" to which Luther says the signs of the church point.

Public prayer includes hymns, liturgy, and other forms of prayer. It is our singing of the psalms, our intercession for those in need, our praying of the Lord's Prayer and our greeting one another in the name of Christ. In all these things, we are participating in the countercultural actions of expressing wonder, asking for what we need, and offering thanksgiving.

Expressing wonder

The Westminster Catechism, a confessional writing of Presbyterians, begins with the question, "What is the chief end of man?" and then the answer, "The chief end of man is to glorify God and enjoy him forever." So, are we having fun yet? The testimony of this confession of faith is that we are supposed to be. Humanity is made for praise, glory, and joy in the presence of God. The third verse of the hymn "Blessing and Honor" makes this point by imagining our lives taking place where praise and love flow freely between heaven and earth:

> Ever ascending the song and the joy
> Ever descending the love from on high;
> Blessing and honor and glory and praise—
> This is the theme of the hymns that we raise;
> This is the theme of the hymns that we raise.[3]

As glorious as this vision is, is it where we live from day to day? Various things can push wonder out of our line of sight. Maybe it is need, or pain, or tragedy. For many of us, the awesome expanse of the universe can shrink to the size of a toothache if the sore tooth is inside your own head. It's all you can think about. How much more can experiences and news of tragedy, danger, and disease in our world break our spirits for joy and wonder!

Of course, an incapacity for wonder does not mean an incapacity for prayer. Lament psalms like that one quoted by Jesus on the cross demonstrate that "the song where we belong" is not always sung in a major key with a cheerful beat. "How long, O Lord?" is a prayer. "My God, my God, why have you forsaken me?" is a prayer.

Life's profound difficulties can change our prayer, but probably more dangerous for a prayerful way of life is something other than tragedy. Most debilitating for glorifying and enjoying God is just the fact that "life happens." Days fill up with small events, duties, and responsibilities until we have succumbed to the temptation, as Annie Dillard says, "to diddle around making itsy-bitsy friends and meals and journeys for itsy-bitsy years on end."[4] We just don't notice anything anymore. I once heard the Lutheran writer and teacher Gerhard Frost comment that he had asked a rancher how sheep get lost. "It's easy," the rancher replied. "They just put their heads down and nibble themselves lost."

In a book on the strengths that congregations have to share with their communities, Gary Gunderson tells the story of noticing one of his days and praying it the way one might pray a psalm.

> I think of one Sunday morning when I got up early to walk the rocky path down into the Grand Canyon. I made it several miles down the trail and climbed up on a rock and listened to the nearly silent wind, which was moving gently through the morning just strongly enough to attract the attention of several hawks who were drifting in the wind about a hundred yards to the west and below. I tasted the dust on the wind thinking that it dated back to Creation, and that placed a different context on my forty-six-year-old aspirations and disappointments. I prayed with my eyes wide open, watching the vastness of time and process. But mostly I listened and thought that maybe I should spend more time watching and listening.[5]

The public prayer of congregations is practice for a life of watching and listening with a sense of wonder.

Voicing need

Prayer is also asking. It is asking for what we need, and asking on behalf of others. According to the prophet Isaiah, God sounds like a child who is eager to be found in a game of hide and seek. "I was ready to be sought out by those who did not ask, to be found by those who did not seek me. I said, 'Here I am! Here I am!' to a nation that did not call on my name" (Isaiah 65:1). "Ask, seek, knock . . . " Jesus tells his disciples; and the prayer that Jesus teaches his disciples speaks one need after another to God: Give us this day our daily bread. Lead us not into temptation. Forgive us our sins as we forgive those who sin against us (cf. Matthew 6:9-13). Three times in one speech, as Jesus is saying good-bye to the disciples, he says, "Ask!" (see John 14:14, 15:7, 16:23-24).

Even so, some things in our way of encountering the world block this form of prayer in daily life, too. Years ago, I heard a corporate coach and psychologist speaking to a small group of coworkers. She was trying to teach the group how to write affirmations for ourselves and give words of affirmation to one another. To show us what she meant, she offered an example of an affirmation that applied to her life. "I can be strong and still have needs," she said. We stared blankly at her. What language was she speaking, exactly? I can be *strong* . . . and still have *needs*? Isn't strength the absence of need?

Admitting need generally compromises strength in processes of negotiation. People telling us how to bargain on a car will say, "Never get so attached to a vehicle that you can't walk away from it. You don't *need* that particular car." Admitting need can also mean giving an unscrupulous conversation partner—or life partner—an edge. If I admit what I need from you, then you know exactly what to withhold if you want to hurt me.

In her novel *Other Women*, Lisa Alther tells the story of Caroline Kelley, a 35-year-old ER nurse burdened by the suffering in the world, who is beginning psychotherapy with Hannah Burke.

> Hannah asks, "So how do you feel about our working together?"
>
> "How do you?" Caroline certainly wasn't going to express interest first. One of her earliest memories was of Maureen, the orange-haired maid from Galway, hissing at her in her crib, "I know what you want and you can't have it!" Caroline couldn't recall what she'd wanted, but she'd learned since that you don't show what you want, because then you deprive others of the satisfaction of denying it to you. You had no business wanting anything anyway if you had food on the table and a roof over your head, when half the world lacked even that."[6]

Can we admit that we need anything from anyone? Wouldn't that be dangerous?

Some people hesitate to voice needs—or anger associated with unmet needs—to God because it appears ungrateful or even disrespectful. Jewish and Christian traditions of prayer are a great help here. The book of Psalms includes almost every kind of prayer one can imagine needing to say. Here are a few examples. There are psalms that praise God (7, 19), psalms to dance to (150), psalms that tell the story of God's salvation (78, 136), psalms that pray for deliverance from enemies, illness, and death (6, 9, 13, 30), as well as psalms that express red-hot anger (137) and a thirst for vindication (54)—and all this is spoken directly to God. In the New Testament, the only kind of prayer God does not seem to like is prayer that one does in order to be seen by others (as in Matthew 6:1-6) or prayer that itemizes someone else's sin in order to make one's own record look good by comparison (as in Luke 18:9-14). Otherwise, all sorts of prayers—even things like, "I believe; help my unbelief!" (Mark 9:24) and "Lord, even the dogs eat the crumbs that fall from their masters' table!" (Matthew 15:27)—receive a favorable hearing.

It is true that sometimes God says "No" to some prayer requests. The most famous "No" to prayer in the New Testament may be the one that the apostle Paul narrates in 2 Corinthians. He explains that he sought relief from a mysterious and unnamed "thorn in the flesh." Three times he prayed, and the answer to his prayer was simple, "My grace is sufficient for you, for power is made perfect in weakness" (2 Corinthians 12:9). Paul's testimony about this is that the Lord who answers this way is not being peevish ("I know what you want, and you can't have it!"), but is, instead, keeping Paul from "being too elated" at his special status as one to whom the glories of heaven have been revealed. The thorn in the flesh keeps Paul's feet on the ground. It keeps him able to tell the story of the Crucified and Risen One; it frees him from the temptation to abandon the story of Jesus in order to regale people with his own remarkable autobiography and his own amazing trips to the third heaven (cf. 2 Corinthians 12:1-10). Without generalizing from Paul's explanation for his own circumstances to an explanation for all negatively answered prayer requests, it is interesting that Paul finds grace and an assurance of ongoing provision even in the "No." "My grace is sufficient for you," he hears and bears witness to, in order for the rest of us to hear.

Offering thanksgiving

If it is countercultural to express wonder (who has time to notice the world around us?) and to admit need (doesn't need look like weakness?), it is equally countercultural to recognize that something good has come to us undeserved. Surely it is a strong work ethic and hours of tireless service that have got us where we are. If anything, we deserve more money or recognition or gratitude for our contributions. In the ministry—perhaps in other types of work as well—it is sadly common for people to work more than they should and then become annoyed when those for whom they work are not sufficiently grateful for all the sacrifices made for them.

Prayers of thanksgiving turn this situation upside down. For a moment, we shift the focus from what we are not getting to all that we have received. I remember a long talk with my car mechanic late at night. It happened that I had to have the car fixed as soon as possible, so Charlie had stayed late to work on it. After dark and with two sleeping kids in the back seat of her car, Charlie's wife, Carol, had come to my house to pick me up and take me to the shop, where my repaired car was waiting. Carol left to get the children home to bed, and I sat down at the side of a dingy metal desk to write a check. As I did that, I asked Charlie, "How did you get your own shop?" My question inspired a 20-minute testimony to God's provision in his life. He started with his boyhood interest in cars, then moved to his work in his back yard as a bona fide "shade tree mechanic," and on to the circumstances that made it possible for him eventually to buy the shop where he and a couple of other guys worked. Along the way, he spoke about Carol, their marriage, their children, Carol's work, the Methodist church they attended ("Music is my worship," he volunteered). The guy was grateful. It was as if everything was a gift to him. Years later, I am still amazed at the exchange. Charlie's words to me were a prayer of thanksgiving offered with the incense of motor oil vapors and the flicker of two fluorescent bulbs in the ceiling of the garage's anteroom.

In 1 Thessalonians 5:17, Paul counsels, "Pray without ceasing." I remember thinking as a child that his exhortation was impossible to carry out. How could anyone pray that much? With the help of people like Gary Gunderson, praying as he watched the hawks and tasted the dust of the Grand Canyon, and with the help of my mechanic, praying as he told the story of finding his calling and being able to make a living at it, I am learning that prayer without ceasing is indeed possible. Saying thanks, voicing need, expressing wonder: we practice these things in Sunday worship as a dress rehearsal for the rest of the week.

> Ever ascending the song and the joy
> Ever descending the love from on high;
> Blessing and honor and glory and praise—
> This is the theme of the hymns that we raise;
> This is the theme of the hymns that we raise.[7]

Questions for discussion

1. Of the three types of prayer discussed in this chapter—expressing wonder, voicing need, and giving thanks—which one is easiest for you? Which one is hardest? Why?
2. Did anyone ever teach you to pray out loud? If so, who was it, and how did they do it?
3. What kind of music do you like in church? Why?

8

The Cross: The Shadow Where We Belong

In the 10th Chapter of Mark, the disciples James and John approach Jesus with a request. "We want you to do for us whatever we ask of you," they begin. "Grant that we may sit, one at your right hand and one at your left, when you come into your glory" (Mark 10:36-37). They are lobbying for cabinet positions in the new administration, and frankly, those of us who have followed the story up to this point have reason to believe they are already on the short list. A few times in the Gospel, Jesus leaves behind all his followers except Peter, James, and John, and the three accompany him on particularly important work. James and John are in the inner circle. So they ask Jesus to make it official. When the time comes, they want their insider status to be formalized.

Jesus conducts a brief job interview with them. "Are you able to drink the cup that I drink, or to be baptized with the baptism that I am baptized with?" The brothers reply with the confidence of overdressed young men greeting the HR staff with a firm handshake and good eye contact, "We are able."

I admire their assurance, but I'm also a little scared for them. If you have heard the story of Jesus before, you know that it is not such a good idea asking to land on the right and the left of Jesus as he is lifted up to reign. At only one other place in the Gospel is any mention made of those on Jesus' right and left. Describing the scene of Jesus' death, the evangelists tell us that Jesus was crucified between two thieves, one on his right, and one on his left.

James and John leave the encounter without the promise of title, rank, or position. Instead, Jesus closes the interview by saying that the brothers will, in fact, drink the cup that he is to drink, but it is not his to grant who will have positions at his right and left.

So what is this cup language about? We hear it one more time in the Gospel. On the verge of his arrest, Jesus prays in Gethsemane, asking not to be required to endure the suffering that is about to befall him. He says, "Abba, Father, for you all things are possible; remove this cup from me; yet, not what I want, but what you want" (Mark 14:36). The cup that Jesus quizzes James and John about is probably the cup of suffering endured on account of one's faithfulness. It is because Jesus is staying faithful to the will of God ("not what I want, but what you want") that he is about to suffer so horribly.

Martin Luther ends his list of ways "a poor confused person" can find the holy Christian people on earth by saying, in effect, look for that kind of faithfulness. Look for the cross. Look for people enduring persecution, hardship, danger, and death precisely because they will not compromise their faithfulness to God.

The history of Christianity is filled with stories of people who have endured astonishing hardship and suffering because their faithfulness to God required them to break step with the powers around them. In the Roman Empire, Christians had to decide whether offering a pinch of incense before the image of the emperor or eating meat that had been butchered in temples dedicated to other gods were gestures of broken faith with the God in whom they trusted. Decisions against eating such meat could cause offense to one's neighbors. A decision against honoring the emperor—in whatever way the emperor wanted to be honored—could result in summary execution at the hands of the state.

Sometimes common, everyday people offer dramatic resistance to things that are wrong and destructive, and both their resistance and their suffering are visible. Then we can see this mark of the body of Christ. Someone is fired for refusing the boss's directive to behave unethically at work. Someone blows the whistle on an abusive church worker and is shunned by a congregation who would prefer to ignore the abuse.

Other times, this public mark of the church is not so public. In fact, one of the problems with finding examples of suffering for the faith in the everyday lives of most of the people I know is that both the depth of their suffering and the tenacity of their faithfulness in spite of it are deeply personal and therefore often private.

A woman loses two young adult children, one to illness and another to violence. She continues to pray, to write, and to speak in ways that bear witness to her devotion to God. I have no idea what she continues to endure daily until she says to me one day, "Sometimes the only prayer we have is, 'My God, my God, why hast thou forsaken me?'"

It is the late 1980s, and a North Dakota farmer is explaining his work to his pastor. We have just been through back-to-back drought years, and the Federal government is offering some relief. The farmer says, offhandedly, "You know, I got so little off this field that I could probably call it a total loss, but there's a ten year-old who works beside me every day. What would I be telling him if I just put the crop in the bin and didn't report it?" We know what he would be telling his son: that cheating is okay if it is the government you're cheating, or, small dishonesty is not really dishonesty, or, that Dad cares more about money than about telling the truth.

Does the lack of a little extra cash qualify as suffering on account of faithfulness to God? Telling the truth about something like this may not immediately seem to be a statement of faith—a turning to God from idols—but the story has stuck with me for years, and I see in it an astonishing willingness to trust God at a time when the present was difficult and the future was uncertain. My friend was a farmer. It had not rained in months. How much faith must he have had to refuse to "work the angles" for a little extra income? Simply telling the truth became a testimony to faith and to the hope that God would make a way, somehow.

And will God make a way? Will the faithful be vindicated? When? How? How long, O Lord?

In the Gospel of Luke, Jesus himself addresses the question of suffering for the faith and God's response to it. "Will not God grant justice to his chosen ones who cry to him day and night? Will he delay long in helping them?" (Luke 18:7-8). Jesus answers his own questions by saying, "I tell you, he will quickly grant justice to them." God will not delay, Jesus says. God will grant justice speedily to those who cry out to him day and night.

That is his answer. Jesus believes that about God. When Jesus says this, of course, he is still outside Jerusalem. He is still at some distance from his own crying out to God at night, in Gethsemane, and by day, on the cross. Does he know yet how dangerously unjust life on this planet can get? If he does not, he is on his way to finding out.

When Jesus finds out about justice and injustice from teachers like Pilate and Herod and crowds of average people like us who had been devoted to him days before his death and then started shouting, "Crucify him!" still, even then, Jesus lives the kind of trust he spoke. Jesus keeps faith with the one from whom he expected vindication. He keeps faith all the way to his death.

When he does this, Jesus gives us a paradox. In the cross, Jesus gives us our clearest picture of the hidden God. God does not peek out from behind the clouds even for a moment and say to the people torturing his son, "Cut it out, down there." The God in whom Jesus trusted, the one who had been positively loquacious at Jesus' baptism, speaking from heaven and all that: "You are my Son, the Beloved; with you I am well pleased"—the God who is supposed to grant justice quickly to his chosen ones who cry out to him: as Jesus cries out, God is silent.

What a strange symbol to have at the center of our faith! A cross. A daily reminder of God's dawdling to grant justice to God's elect.

What a strange symbol . . . unless justice is something different from what we expect. In the cross, Jesus gives us our clearest picture of God hidden and silent. But also in the cross—and this is the paradox—Jesus gives us our clearest picture of God's true self, and of God's way of bringing about justice. God, our sovereign God, the creator of heaven and earth, the God who is greater than all—God does not, in the service of justice, reach for a bigger hammer. God, in the person of Jesus Christ, picks up a cross. Jesus lays down his life for friends and enemies alike, and when he does that, Jesus shows us that God's justice is inextricably bound up with God's own suffering love. Military officers know you cannot save a village by destroying it. God does not attempt to save the lost by destroying them. God seeks and saves the lost by remaining connected to them with a love strong enough to resist evil in all its forms.

The National Public Radio show *All Things Considered* reported the story of a woman testifying shortly before a death penalty sentence was to be carried out. She testified on the side of clemency for the man who killed her father and stepmother. (The transcript of the interview, which aired on May 27, 2003, is available at http://soundportraits.org/on-air/clemency/transcript.php3.)

> At the hearing, Sue Norton told the clemency panel, "Few of you will ever be able to experience or understand the depth of the pain that I felt as I knelt down cleaning up the blood of my daddy." She went on to describe what happened to her after the trial and how she came to know her parents' murderer and finally to ask for his life to be spared. She told the interviewer, "During the trial, they put me on the witness stand, and at the very end, he said, 'How did you know Richard and Virginia Denney?' And I just burst out bawling, and I said, 'It's my daddy and my stepmother!' When I looked over at the jury, every single one of them was crying. They gave Robert Knighton the death penalty for me.

> "The last day of the trial, I went to bed crying. And I just prayed and asked God, you know, What on earth [am] I supposed to be feeling? When I woke, the thought in my head was, Sue you could forgive him. That really was a message from God."

> Norton visited Robert Knighton in prison, and recalled their first conversation this way. "I saw him at the jail in November of 1990. All of the sudden I'm standing in front of this big guy. The only thing between us was the bars. I was shaking like a leaf and looked at him and I said, 'I don't know what to say to you, except I want you to know that I don't hate you.' He said, 'You should. You'd be better off.' And I said, 'No, I've not ever hated anyone in my whole life, and I'm not going start today.'"

One can hear in Norton's story the *resistance* that is part of suffering love. Love like this is harder even than the work of nurturing a sense of righteous indignation or of "shutting off" one's feelings toward another. The cross demonstrates a kind of love that speaks *no* as forcefully as yes. "No," she says. "I've not ever hated anyone in my whole life, and I'm not going start today."

Christians confess that the clearest visual evidence of that deep, tenacious, evil-resistant love is the weakened, crumpled, dying figure of Christ crucified. One of the marks of the church, one piece of visual evidence pointing to the Christian church on earth is that—sometimes in small ways and sometimes in grand, dramatic ways—evil continues to be resisted by means of love.

Questions for discussion

1. Have you seen love resisting evil in the world? If so, share examples that come to mind.
2. Where does the courage come from to resist returning hurt for hurt?
3. How does the cross help you understand the suffering of Sue Norton at the loss of her parents? How does it help you understand her forgiving Robert Knighton?

9

Belonging Together: Community, Risk, and the Presence of Christ

There is a danger with the title of this book. A phrase like "signs of belonging" can conjure up images of a clubhouse, a college fraternity or sorority, or some other kind of members-only association. Sometimes we human beings speak of belonging precisely in order to differentiate ourselves from those outside our group. We and our preferred associates are in. Others don't belong.

Is that what it means to belong to a group that is recognized by the preaching of the Word, by the practices of Baptism and Holy Communion, by forgiveness, ministry and worship, and by its suffering on account of faithfulness to God? Are these "signs of belonging" the means by which Christians form a tidy, cozy fellowship of people like just like ourselves?

The biblical stories we have looked at point in a different direction. In these stories, boundaries between groups of people are not reinforced, but redefined, and community comes to mean a collection of people like us, and people different from us. What's more, it is not coziness that characterizes these stories, but rather risk. Finally, the living presence of Christ in the stories means that tidiness gives way to unexpected, unmerited grace, as God uses the church to show the world what God's reign looks like.

Community

For a moment, it looks like the woman who anoints Jesus with perfume does not belong in the story she has just entered, yet Jesus defends her actions and gives her and her actions a permanent place in the story. Paul tells Philemon and Onesimus, who have known each other as master and slave, that they are brothers. In Revelation, John witnesses people from every nation, tribe, and language gathered around the throne of the Lamb, offering praise.

If you are a member of a Christian congregation, imagine what it might mean for that group of people to be shaped the way community is shaped in these stories. I remember a sermon about the meaning of Christian community, in which the preacher commented on something he had noticed earlier in the week. Once a month, church members served dinner at a homeless shelter. The pastor had seen something at the shelter: parishioners were friendly to the homeless men who were going through the line to receive dinner. Everyone was friendly, the pastor said, but he wondered whether we had noticed something about the way we related to the men at the shelter. "Did you notice that we all stayed on our side of the serving table, and they all stayed on their side?" he asked us during the sermon. "I wonder what it might be like for us to mix that up a little?"

Where are the divisions between "us" and "them" in your congregation or in the ministry you do? Maybe the divide exists between clergy and laity, or between the older women and younger women, or between those who attend the traditional worship service and those who attend the contemporary service. Maybe the divide is between church members who drive in from other neighborhoods to attend "our church," and a neighborhood populated by people with a different language, nationality, or background from that of the people in the pews on Sunday morning. What things exist to keep those divisions in place? What might break down the barriers? What would it be like for you to mix that up a little?

Risk

No one in the biblical stories we have read is playing it safe. The woman with expensive ointment risks—and receives—ridicule as she anoints Jesus. Zacchaeus risks the same thing as he, a dignified rich man, hikes up his robe and runs ahead of the crowd, climbing a tree so that he can see Jesus. Jesus himself risks alienating righteous people when he goes to Zacchaeus's house to eat; everyone knows that Zacchaeus is a sinner and a collaborator with the Romans. Onesimus, the slave, risks going home to a master who may punish him, or even kill him, instead of receiving him as a beloved brother in Christ.

What on earth has gotten into these people? Why aren't they more careful? Is the Christian life inherently reckless?

When I moved to North Dakota I was initiated into life on the prairie with stories about the danger of blizzards. Anytime after the autumnal equinox, I was told, it was unwise to venture away from home without a blanket, matches, a candle in an empty coffee can, and some chocolate bars in the back of my car. Then, if I were stranded, I could stay warm, melt snow for water to drink, and consume small portions of high calorie food until someone found me. As one woman was telling me about the survival kit and its contents, she related how her daughters never paid any attention to their parents' concerns when they left home in the winter. They would drive to far away high school basketball games with no survival gear in the car. Their recklessness frustrated their mother, but their dad had said, "The girls aren't careless. They're just carefree."

Maybe the people in the biblical stories are not careless as much as they are carefree. Zacchaeus and the woman with the alabaster jar of ointment focused on Jesus to the extent that other cares do not matter to them. Having been introduced to the story of Jesus, Onesimus finds the courage to take Paul's letter back to Philemon and trust that he will receive a welcome home. Jesus himself cannot be bothered by concern for the sensibilities of the righteous. He has come "to seek out and to save the lost" (Luke 19:10). These people are free of the cares that might have bound them to a safer way of life.

Is there anything reckless—or carefree—about the way people in your congregation practice their faith? Maybe you have heard discussions at annual meetings about the church budget. How much money in the bank is enough? Is it safe to begin a new type of ministry? That is, will the church building, or the bank accounts, or the lawn, or the parking lot be able to sustain the new venture? Or, is it safe to put our faith into action away from the church? Should we really go to the capitol and talk to legislators about housing, education, or peace? What if we offend some people? I don't usually think of going to church as a risk, but maybe it is. Is it risky where you live? What trouble might you get into?

The presence of Christ

Each of the marks of the church—and each of the stories that describe them here—has Jesus at its center. Jesus is the object of the devotion of the woman with perfume. It is as a result of baptism into Christ that Philemon and Onesimus are brothers. As Zacchaeus sits at table with Jesus, something happens to change him. The frightened disciples hear that they have the authority to forgive sins when Jesus says to them: "as the Father has sent me, so I send you." The disciples are able to feed 5000 people because of what happens when Jesus takes five loaves and two fish, blesses them, breaks them, and gives them to the disciples to distribute. Worship, in Revelation, is centered around the throne of the Lamb, who is the risen Lord Jesus. Finally, Jesus says to James and John that they will drink the cup of suffering that he will endure on the cross. The Word, Baptism, Holy Communion, forgiveness, ministry, worship, and suffering for the faith: each of these is a sign of the presence of Christ in the world.

A Christian congregation, then, is not a sanctuary from the world, but a window on what God, in Christ, is doing in the world. God's work in the world is often hidden. Yet, as God's people participate in the signs of the church, people inside and outside the church get a glimpse of God's reign. That reign is characterized by risk, by relationships that are redefined in Christ and renewed by forgiveness, by motley groups of people singing praise to the Lamb, and by love that overcomes evil with good. Can you see these things in your life? Can you see them in your congregation? If so, you are seeing the work of God in and for the world.

Questions for discussion

1. Where do you experience a sense of community? What makes you feel welcome in a new place?

2. Do you find it risky to be a Christian? If so, where and when? What trouble might you get into because you are a Christian?

3. Of the seven marks of the church, are there certain ones that are particularly meaningful or important to you? If so, why?

Resources for Further Study

Carter, Jimmy. *Living Faith*. New York: Random House, 1996.

This book is a memoir about the role that the Christian faith and faith communities have played in former President Carter's life.

Dawn, Marva. *A Royal "Waste" of Time: The Splendor of Worshiping God and Being Church for the World*. Grand Rapids: Eerdmans, 1999.

In this book, Lutheran theologian Marva Dawn has collected essays and sermons that demonstrate the role of worship in forming what Luther called "the Christian holy people" for service and witness in the world.

Dillard, Annie. *Holy the Firm*. New York: Harper & Row, 1977.

Dillard is a Pulitzer prize-winning essayist. *Holy the Firm* is an account of the evidence—and hiddenness—of God in nature written during a two-year residence on Puget Sound.

Gunderson, Gary. *Deeply Woven Roots: Improving the Quality of Life in Your Community*. Minneapolis: Fortress, 1997.

Gary Gunderson directs the Interfaith Health Program, affiliated with the Carter Center and Emory University. *In Deeply Woven Roots*, Gunderson has written an engaging account of the strengths congregations bring to the neighborhoods in which they exist. The IHP website is also an excellent resource: www.ihpnet.org

Lamott, Anne. *Traveling Mercies: Some Thoughts on Faith*. New York: Pantheon, 1999.

Anne Lamott is a writer who came to congregational Christianity as an adult. *Traveling Mercies* is a collection of essays about life, family, love, loss, and faith.

Lischer, Richard. *Open Secrets: A Spiritual Journey through a Country Church.* New York: Doubleday, 2001.

Richard Lischer teaches preaching at Duke Divinity School in Durham, North Carolina. *Open Secrets* is the story of his first call as a Lutheran minister to a congregation in rural Illinois.

Paulson, Steven D. *Luther for Armchair Theologians.* Philadelphia: Westminster/John Knox, forthcoming.

Steven Paulson teaches systematic theology at Luther Seminary in St. Paul, Minnesota. This book is a short introduction to Luther's life and thought, complete with cartoons!

Taylor, Barbara Brown. *The Preaching Life.* Boston: Cowley, 1993.

Barbara Brown Taylor has published a number of volumes of sermons. She is a teacher, preacher, and Episcopal priest. *The Preaching Life* includes both a memoir of how she came to be in ordained ministry and a small collection of sermons.

Notes

Chapter 1: Where Is the Church? Signs of Belonging

1 "On the Councils and the Church," trans. Charles M. Jacobs, *Luther's Works: The American Edition* (Philadelphia: Fortress Press, 1966), 41:148.

2 Ibid., 41:148.

3 Ibid., 41:150.

4 Ibid., 41:154.

5 Ibid., 41:164.

6 Ibid., 41:165f.

Chapter 2: Where is the Church? Signs of Belonging

1 Barbara Brown Taylor, *The Preaching Life* (Boston: Cowley, 1993) 56.

Chapter 3: Holy Baptism: The Bath Where We Belong

1 *Lutheran Book of Worship* (*LBW*) (Minneapolis: Augsburg Fortress, 1978), p. 125.

Chapter 4: Holy Communion: The Table Where We Belong

1 Gail Godwin, *Evensong* (New York: Ballentine Books, 1999), p. 339.

2 Ibid., p. 344.

Chapter 5: Forgiveness and Reproof of Sin: The Truth Where We Belong

1 *LBW*, p. 90.

2 Marcia Witten, *All Is Forgiven* (Princeton: Princeton Univ. Press, 1993), p. 82.

3 Anne Lamott, *Traveling Mercies* (New York: Pantheon, 1999), p. 213.

4 *Service Book and Hymnal* (*SBH*) (Minneapolis: Augsburg, 1958), p. 252.

Chapter 6: The Office of the Ministry: The Care Where We Belong

1 Richard Lischer, "Resurrection and Rhetoric," in *Marks of the Body of Christ*, Carl E. Braaten and Robert W. Jenson, eds. (Grand Rapids: Eerdmans, 1999), p. 16.

2 Andrew Solomon, *The Noonday Demon* (New York: Simon and Schuster, 2001), p. 437.

3 Luther's Works 41:154.

Chapter 7: Worship: The Song Where We Belong

1 *LBW* 525.

2 Ibid., 315.

3 Ibid., 525.

4 Annie Dilliard, *Pilgrim at Tinker Creek* (New York: Bantam Books, 1974), p. 276.

5 Gary Gunderson, *Deeply Woven Roots* (Minneapolis: Fortress, 1997), p. 109.

6 Lisa Alther, *Other Women* (New York: Penguin, 1984), p. 26.

7 *LBW* 525.

OTHER LUTHERAN VOICES TITLES

Large-quantity purchases or custom editions of these books are available at a discount from the publisher. For more information, contact the sales department at Augsburg Fortress, Publishers, 1-800-328-4648, or write to: Sales Director, Augsburg Fortress, Publishers, P.O. Box 1209, Minneapolis, MN 55440-1209.

See www.lutheranvoices.com